EUROPEAN DEFENCE POLICY

European Defence Policy

Beyond the Nation State

FRÉDÉRIC MÉRAND

OXFORD
UNIVERSITY PRESS

OXFORD
UNIVERSITY PRESS

Great Clarendon Street, Oxford OX2 6DP

Oxford University Press is a department of the University of Oxford.
It furthers the University's objective of excellence in research, scholarship,
and education by publishing worldwide in

Oxford New York

Auckland Cape Town Dar es Salaam Hong Kong Karachi
Kuala Lumpur Madrid Melbourne Mexico City Nairobi
New Delhi Shanghai Taipei Toronto

With offices in

Argentina Austria Brazil Chile Czech Republic France Greece
Guatemala Hungary Italy Japan Poland Portugal Singapore
South Korea Switzerland Thailand Turkey Ukraine Vietnam

Oxford is a registered trade mark of Oxford University Press
in the UK and in certain other countries

Published in the United States
by Oxford University Press Inc., New York

© Frédéric Mérand 2008

The moral rights of the author have been asserted
Database right Oxford University Press (maker)

First published in 2008

British Library Cataloguing in Publication Data
Data available

Library of Congress Cataloging in Publication Data
Data available

Typeset by SPI Publisher Services, Pondicherry, India
Printed in Great Britain
on acid-free paper by
Biddles Ltd., King's Lynn, Norfolk

ISBN 978-0-19-953324-4

1 3 5 7 9 10 8 6 4 2

à mes parents
für Maya

Preface

Dying for the European Union? The thought is odd. After all, no one has died for the EU yet, and I certainly wish that no one ever will. But that is what I had in mind while writing this book. In his 1951 masterpiece, *Pro Patria Mori*, Ernst Kantorowicz showed how the medieval Christian notion of absolute sacrifice was secularized and then nationalized in the late Middle Ages, thus reverting to its Roman interpretation of dying for one's political community. Kantorowicz's short text made an immense impression on me because it disentangles so clearly the relations between the state, the military, and citizenship, a topic I have been obsessed with ever since. The present book is an attempt to understand what it means to be a citizen, a statesman, or a soldier in today's EU. The development of the European security and defence policy (ESDP), to this day the most ambitious project of military integration in times of peace, seemed like a good place to start.

Mark Webber (2004: 19) and his colleagues call the Europeanization of security and defence policy "one of the great political revolutions of the late twentieth and early twenty-first centuries." It is indeed a political revolution (albeit an incomplete one) which forces us to rethink the national state–armed forces nexus and more broadly the interplay of national identity and the state. This political revolution I approach with a very specific conception of political sociology, a mixture of Weberian and Durkheimian traditions that we find in the works of Pierre Bourdieu, but also Michael Mann, Charles Tilly, Karl Deutsch, and Norbert Elias. This reflects my own theoretical sensibility and my academic training, which is grounded in the political sociology of the state, and state formation in particular. But I think most political sociologists will recognize themselves in the research strategy I have pursued, which begins by questioning the social categories, like the "state," "rationality," "identity," and "interests," that are often taken for granted in International Relations and European integration theory. Political sociologists will also, I hope, share my concern for empirical research. While political commentary and abstract formalization are not useless, it is also important to get as close as possible to the research object, to immerse oneself in it, to familiarize oneself with the social practices that underpin it, while keeping the distance that is necessary to contextualize what social actors apprehend as their "common sense."

The book comes out of a PhD dissertation completed at the University of California, Berkeley. I thank my dissertation committee: Neil Fligstein, a mentor and a friend, whose theoretical influence in the following pages will be obvious to anyone who is familiar with his work; Gil Eyal, because if there remain any conceptual gaps, it is certainly not because he failed to point them out to me; and Christopher Ansell, who helped me pitch the argument at a level that will hopefully be comprehensible to both sociologists and International Relations scholars.

The late Pierre Bourdieu warned us relentlessly against the perils of *skholè*, the scholastic disposition that creates an artificial distance between the observer and his "social object." Yet, *skholè* also means leisure, and I was fortunate enough to find colleagues who, beyond the call of duty, took the time to read and comment on the manuscript. In particular, I am grateful to Bastien Irondelle, Stephanie Hofmann, Cornelia Woll, Christoph Meyer, Hanna Ojanen, Martin Schain, Greggor Mattson, Liesbet Hooghe, Michel Fortmann, Martial Foucault, Virginie Guiraudon, Juan Diez Medrano, Craig Parsons, David Spence, Marcos Ancelovici, Vincent Pouliot, Brian Rathbun, and two anonymous reviewers from Oxford University Press. Jolyon Howorth deserves special thanks: for my generation of European security scholars, Howorth's insightful publications on ESDP were mandatory reading. Although we do not agree on everything, my research would have been impossible without the crucial information he uncovered and the paths of inquiry he laid out for us.

I also wish to register my appreciation to the 40 odd politicians, government officials, and military officers who were kind enough to spend some of their precious time answering my candid questions. (In keeping with my ethical commitments, interviewees are never identified in the text unless they agreed to it.) I became so fascinated with their work that I was the victim of a Freudian transfer and joined the Canadian foreign ministry in 2004–5. I thank my colleagues in Ottawa for making this "postdoctoral ethnography" so enjoyable, and also for gracefully agreeing to let me go back to my real home, academia.

This research was made possible thanks to generous fellowships from the Institute of International Studies, the Institute on Global Conflict and Cooperation, and the Centre for Culture, Organizations and Politics, all at the University of California, as well as the Social Science and Humanities Research Council and the Quebec Research Fund on Society and Culture. At my new home, the University of Montreal, I depended a lot on a great team of graduate students: Haingo Rakotonirina, Mathieu Ferland, Marc-André Viau, Stéfanie von Hlatky, Alexandre Carette, Joëlle Dumouchel, Antoine Vandemoortele, and Julie Auger.

This book is dedicated to my "little love," Maya Jegen, who carefully read the manuscript and purged it of much of its heaviness, and to my parents, Francine Boulé and Yves Mérand, who shared not only their love but also their cultural capital, which as a political sociologist I am grateful for. They were both the necessary and the sufficient condition for this to ever appear in print.

Outremont
September 2007

Contents

Tables and Figures

Tables

Figures

Abbreviations

AU	African Union
CFSP	common foreign and security policy
COCOR	Coordination of the Council of Ministers
COPS	Political and Security Committee
COREPER	Committee of Permanent Representatives
COREU	Correspondance européenne
CPCO	Centre de planification et de conduite des opérations
CSCE	Conference on Security and Cooperation in Europe
DCI	Defence Capabilities Initiative
DPC	Defence Planning Committee
ECAP	European Capabilities Action Plan
ECSC	European Coal and Steel Community
EDA	European Defence Agency
EDC	European Defence Community
EEC	European Economic Community
EMIA	Etat-major interarmées
EPC	European Political Cooperation
ESDI	European security and defence identity
ESDP	European security and defence policy
EU	European Union
EUFOR	EU Military Force
EUMC	EU Military Committee
EUMS	EU Military Staff
EURATOM	European Atomic Energy Community
EUROFOR	European Rapid Operational Force
EUROMARFOR	European Maritime Force
FAWEU	Forces Answerable to WEU

FCO	Foreign and Commonwealth Office
GDP	gross domestic product
IGC	Intergovernmental conference
NATO	North Atlantic Treaty Organization
OCCAR	Organisation conjointe de coopération en matière d'armements
OSCE	Organization for Security and Cooperation in Europe
PJHQ	Permanent Joint Headquarters
QMV	qualified majority voting
SACEUR	Supreme Allied Commander, Europe
SACT	Supreme Allied Commander Transformation
SHAPE	Supreme Headquarters Allied Powers, Europe
UN	United Nations
UNGA	UN General Assembly
WEU	Western European Union

Introduction

State formation in Western Europe was a process by which rulers forcibly accumulated, concentrated, and centralized capital and means of coercion away from smaller units, thus creating national states (Tilly 1992). European integration, however, is characterized by an apparent willingness on the part of today's rulers to pool and sometimes delegate their authority over capital and coercion to a larger entity, the European Union (EU). This transformation of the European state, one of the most puzzling political phenomena of the late twentieth century, has been well studied so far as capital is concerned. For reasons that are well understood, if debated, the regulation of economic power is now firmly located in Brussels' Berlaymont, the seat of the European Commission, and the European Central Bank's Eurotower, in Frankfurt.

For a time, the question of coercion did not seem to elicit similar interest. It was assumed that the regional integration of Europe was driven by economic considerations and would hardly lend itself to high politics (Hoffmann 1966). The EU played a role in security affairs, since its existence had arguably contributed to preventing armed conflicts on the western part of the continent after World War II. But Brussels did not properly speaking claim a right, in Max Weber's words, to monopolize legitimate means of coercion. In this book, I show that this is changing, and that there are ways to explain it.

The dream of a European army is much older than the EU. Already in the seventeenth century, the Duke de Sully, Henri IV's finance minister, made detailed plans for a continental army of 270,000 infantrymen, 50,000 cavalrymen, 200 cannons, and 120 warships. This force, overseen by a "Christian Council," could have been used to solve conflicts among European nations and enforce common rules. A few decades later, the American William Penn, in his *Essay towards the Present and Future Peace in Europe, by the Establishment of an European Dyet, Parliament, or Estates* and the French Abbott of Saint-Pierre, in his *Projet pour rendre la paix perpétuelle en Europe*, took up the idea. For Saint-Pierre, who wrote his *Projet* in 1712, the "European Union" should have a multinational army to defend its "society." Needless to say, none of these ambitious ideas ever came to fruition.

In the contemporary era, the project of a European military organization goes back to 1950, when the architects of the European Coal and Steel Community (ECSC), the ancestor of the EU, designed a European Defence Community (EDC) to complement it. Following the ECSC's federal approach, the EDC would have been composed of multinational military forces from France, Germany, Italy, and the Benelux countries, overseen by a supranational authority and a European defence minister. Agreed upon by the six founding members of the coal and steel "pool" in 1952, the EDC fell into oblivion when the French National Assembly failed in 1954 to ratify the Treaty of Paris. Thereafter, the US-led North Atlantic Treaty Organization (NATO) took on security issues in the face of the Soviet threat, while what became the EU in 1993 focused on economic matters.

The idea of a truly autonomous defence organization resurfaced in the early 1990s in the wake of the EU's new common foreign and security policy (CFSP). The Treaty of Maastricht even cautiously mentioned the "eventual framing of a common defence policy, which might in time lead to a common defence." Yet this led to little or no action, in large part due to British resistance. The 40-year taboo was only really broken in 1998 when, at the Franco-British summit held in St. Malo, the EU's two military powers agreed to launch a joint initiative that eventually became the European security and defence policy (ESDP).

ESDP, enshrined in the 2001 Treaty of Nice, is not a single policy like the EU's external trade policy, where the Commission enjoys supranational competence. It is not a collective defence pact like the North Atlantic Treaty either, let alone an integrated European army like the one envisaged in the stillborn EDC. Yet, in a way, ESDP is more unsettling of national defence postures than NATO and the EDC were. While highly integrated militarily, NATO was and remains a defensive alliance in the tradition of realist international relations. The EDC was also wedded to a traditional conception of state sovereignty, whereby states came together to defend themselves against a known enemy, the Soviet Union. ESDP, by contrast, is not geared towards a particular threat in specific historical circumstances. Its objective is not national defence, but political integration, which encompasses the institutional development of Europe, the formation of a European identity, and the creation of region-wide industrial champions in the defence sector. Once EU states have agreed that they should coordinate their defence policies not for territorial self-defence but for *political* reasons—namely, to support a common foreign policy and usher in the political integration of Europe—it makes little sense to say that the instruments of legitimate coercion remain a privilege of the national state. Because it touches upon the core of state sovereignty, ESDP redefines the nature of European integration and the way we think about the state in the twenty-first century.

The fact that, without external threat, a large number of political leaders, military officers, and diplomats are willing, at least in principle, to partly surrender a key element of their state identity—the link between national defence and the state—suggests that there is something other than collective defence or state-making at stake. The proponents of a common defence policy are neither militarists trying to create a new alliance against some threat nor ardent federalists trying to replicate the experience of national state formation. One argument made in this book is that, in contrast to failed past experiences, European defence has become rather uncontroversial, and that this lack of controversy says something about the state of the European state. Indeed, in Europe today it is considered quite *normal* to be in favour of common defence: 85% of the Germans, 81% of the French, and an astounding 59% of the British support a common defence policy.[1] Such numbers are not only unthinkable in any other regional organization, they are also considerably higher than support for membership in the EU *itself*, which reaches 58% in Germany, 51% in France, and 36% in the UK. Across the EU, 54% of the people support membership of their country, while 77% support a common defence policy.

Defence policy has gone beyond the nation state. High public support for—or at least public indifference towards—European defence has created a historically unprecedented political space for bureaucratic elites to experiment and enact new forms of transnational governance. But the puzzle remains of why these actors decided to do so.

---

[1] Eurobarometer 63, 2005.

MILITARY INTEGRATION AND THE TRANSFORMATION
OF THE STATE

The premise of this book is that European defence can be analysed with the tools of political sociology. More specifically, I explain the emergence and consolidation of ESDP as part of a broader transformation of the European state, whereby its Weberian definition as a political organization whose "administrative staff successfully upholds the claim to the monopoly of the legitimate use of physical force in the enforcement of its order" is put to a serious challenge (Weber 1978: 54–6). But, I will argue, the challenge derives less from the forces of globalization or some "regional integration logic" than from the intentional but constrained actions of state actors, and precisely those who are seen as the carriers of state sovereignty: statesmen, diplomats, and military officers. Instead of showing government preferences, state interests, or macro-changes as causes, I explore why state actors from different countries came to work together, and how their cooperation became stable over time.

There is today a great deal of social interaction between security and defence actors in Europe. That is because ESDP has led to the creation of a European security and defence *field*, where these state actors are in constant interaction with each other. This level of interaction is unique in the West and yet it is the result neither of the aggregation of national preferences nor of supranational entrepreneurship. Rather, the transgovernmental field—I will have more to say about this concept below—that has emerged in Europe is a by-product of two parallel developments that have been unfolding since the end of World War II and are peculiar to Europe: the internationalization of European defence structures and the Europeanization of foreign policymaking.[2] These developments occurred

---

[2] As Olsen (2002) argues, there are (too) many definitions of Europeanization. It can refer to top–down (downloading from EU to the state), bottom–up (uploading from states to the EU), or transversal (from state to state) processes. Caporaso, Cowles, and Risse (2001: 3) define Europeanization as "the emergence of and the development at the European level of distinct structures of governance" which member states must adapt to. Radaelli (2006: 59), for his part, defines it as interactive "processes of a) construction b) diffusion and c) institutionalization of formal and informal rules, rules, procedures, policy paradigms, styles and 'ways of doing things.'" In contrast to most of the literature, the definition of Europeanization adopted here is not a causal but a *descriptive* one: it refers quite simply to the institutionalization of a social space of interaction whose "effects" are bounded and roughly correspond to the European continent (Bourdieu and Wacquant 1992; Cohen, Dezalay, and Marchetti 2007; Fligstein 2008). Similarly,

against the backdrop of the declining importance of "national defence" in people's definition of the state, at least in Europe. Certain individuals or groups of actors were instrumental in shaping ESDP, but without those structural conditions already in place, there would be no talk of ESDP today.

Now that it is strongly institutionalized, the European security and defence field affects the practices, social representations, and power relations of security and defence actors in a fundamental way. Soldiers and diplomats have increasingly converged towards the EU as a given, as something worth fighting over, and as a "natural" solution to their concerns. This explains why the European defence initiative was able to make significant progress since 1998 despite the political context of institutional crisis that dominated those years, with the botched Nice Treaty, the failed constitutional treaty, bickering over the Iraq war, an economic downturn, and personal animosity between EU leaders. Given the robustness of this transgovernmental field of interaction, it is therefore likely that European defence will sustain further progress even in the absence of strong political leadership.

The argument that I just sketched out requires some historical pointers before I return to it in more detail later. Before the advent of national states, Europe was characterized by regimes of fragmented sovereignty, arguably like the EU today, which is often described as a regime of "multilevel governance." In these times as in later ones, rulers sought to wage wars. But war requires resources. Drawing from Otto Hintze's pioneering historical work, Charles Tilly showed how in the specific context of medieval Europe the necessities of war-making and the requirements of an efficient and large army led, through their interaction with capitalism, to the formation of national states. "War," he wrote, "wove the European network of national states, and preparation for war created the internal structures of the state within it" (Tilly 1985: 76). Tilly subsumed under the rubric of "organized crime" the various strategies used by rulers to extract resources from their constituencies, most notably repression and administration.

Tilly's research has sparked a plethora of work on the military and geopolitical foundations of state-building (Finer 1975; Downing 1992;

"internationalization" would characterize a somewhat broader space, here a transatlantic one since it includes US and Canadian actors—that is why "transatlanticization" may be more appropriate (but less elegant) a term.

Spruyt 1994; Ertman 1997). To maintain strong, permanent, dedicated armies, rulers developed public administrations that would raise taxes and manage supplies; they instated conscription to ensure a steady turnout of manpower; they built railroad and communication systems to increase the mobility of troops; and they supported public education to foster feelings of national belonging. All of these had the effect of creating an intimate connection between armed forces and the national state (Girardet 1998). Paul Hirst (2001: 23) so concludes: "modern war thus implie[d] mass armies and the creation of forms of legitimacy that tie[d] soldiers to the regime."

Of course, the scope of state formation went far beyond the military institution. As Pierre Bourdieu argued, the monopoly on violence that the state claims to hold is as much symbolic as it is physical. "The state," he wrote, "is the culmination of a process of concentration of different kinds of capital: ... coercive capital (army, police), economic capital, cultural or informational capital, and symbolic capital. This concentration, as such, gives the state a sort of meta-capital, which gives it power over the other kinds of capital and their holders" (Bourdieu 1994: 109).

In Bourdieu's sociology, each kind of "capital" is linked to a specific *social field*, a structured space of relations, centred on agreed-upon stakes, functioning according to known if implicit rules, wherein actors draw on their capital as a resource to maintain their position in the field. Thus, there is an economic field, a legal field, a security field, a cultural field, a bureaucratic field, each with its own logic and set of actors.

What Bourdieu says is that the formation of the state can be analysed as the genesis of a field of power. The field of power is where the holders of different kinds of capital compete with each other for control over state authority, which will strengthen their position by creating rules, symbols, and resources that favour them. State formation is thus a process of differentiation and integration. It is a process of differentiation because each social field becomes increasingly complex and autonomous: the economy emancipates itself from political domination; the cultural field is separated from the religious, and so on. And state formation is a process of integration because fields remain interdependent and connected through the "meta-capital" provided by the state. For example, artists become increasingly dependent on the resources and prestige bestowed upon them by state foundations and museums; schools receive the right to offer educational programs through state licenses; defence planners are tied to business firms through state-administered procurement programs. The result is a society in which the state is both *constitutive* of a variety of relatively autonomous fields and *constituted* by the consolidation of these fields and the struggles that take place in them.

This is a useful lens through which to analyse state formation in Western Europe. Between the sixteenth and the nineteenth century, countries like France, Britain, and Prussia saw the emergence of permanent military institutions. Armed forces were professionalized and standardized. To be a soldier became a full-time job, as soldiers were often secluded from the rest of the society. Military activity was routinized, with barracks, standard *matériel*, drills, and maneuvers. The system of ranks was formalized and services (navy, army, etc.) were institutionalized (Huntington 1957; Ralston 1966; Parker 1996). There emerged a stable set of relations among military professionals with clear lines of authority, system of promotion, and mandates. In other words, the military field became increasingly homogenous and autonomous from other social spheres.

In parallel, capitalism was taking off with the growth of national markets, the beginnings of industrial policy, and the creation of corporations. The modern "market" was becoming a complex and relatively autonomous field of interaction. The incipient state was an active player in its creation and development. It came to define who the legitimate actors were, what rules applied, what counted as property, and so on (Bourdieu 2000; Fligstein 2001a). In return, market actors generated economic resources that the state could tap into to fund the unprecedented expansion of its coercive and administrative power.[3]

These two developments, militarization and capitalism, reinforced each other. The nexus of their interdependency was the state. Military leaders needed the resources that only the fiscal state, with its capacity to generate revenue, could provide. Merchants and entrepreneurs needed protection and a stable set or rules (a legal system, property rights, a tariffs policy, infrastructure, etc.) that only the administrative state and its bureaucracy could provide. The state embodied the field of power wherein military and economic leaders vied for control over the resources they needed.

---

[3] What Mann (1993) calls "despotic" and "infrastructural" power. See also Tilly (1992). On the fiscal sociology of the emerging state, see Lindert (2004).

As Tilly argues in *Coercion, Capital and European States*, the national state *à la* France or Britain, with its centralized administration over a fixed territory, became the dominant form of political organization precisely because it was able to both use coercive forces to protect the national market and channel economic resources to support the military. This model more or less became the basis for Weber's classic definition of the state.

Bourdieu makes the additional point that the national state derived a great deal of *symbolic* power from this conjuncture. Social representations became national in that they were homogenized, codified, and imposed by the national state. The state, Bourdieu (1994: 114) argues, "shapes mental structures and imposes principles of vision and division ... thereby contributing to the construction of what is commonly called national identity." Through the school system, military service, civil administration, and the media, "national" frames were impressed upon social conceptions of history, science, religion, and even, as Kantorowicz documents in *Pro Patria Mori*, duty.[4] Millions of people died and continue to die partly because they were coerced to go to war, but also because they were made to believe that, in doing so, they were serving some higher, patriotic, "national" purpose.

In spite of differences in vocabulary, very much the same argument is made by Michael Mann (1986: 1), for whom "societies are constituted of multiple overlapping and intersecting sociospatial networks of power." These networks are like Bourdieu's fields: they are institutionalized spaces of social interaction that constitute *loci* of power. While Bourdieu assumed that there could be as many fields as were actually institutionalized, Mann distinguishes four types of networks that he thinks are found in every society: economic, military, ideological, and political.

Mann draws from Owen Lattimore's 1962 study of the relations between Mongol tribes and China, where the US historian argued that there existed three *radii* of extensive social integration: military action, civil administration, and economic integration. In the Chinese Empire, these *radii* did not have the same width. The reach of military organizations was much larger than that of tradesmen, with civil administration somewhere in

---

[4] On the link between national identity and the school system, see Gellner (1983), who spoke of the state's monopoly over legitimate *education*. On the link between national identity and military service, see Weber (1974). On the link between national identity and the media, see Anderson (1983).

between. Mann adds a fourth *radius* of social integration, the ideological one, and extends Lattimore's argument to show that the four types of network are also sources of unequal power. For example, in medieval Europe, Christendom constituted an ideological network that was more important, extensive, and meaningful than circuits of economic exchange. After the fifteenth century, however, economic and military power relations rose to dominance, as religion became an issue to be ruled domestically by political leaders, especially after the 1555 Peace of Augsburg and the 1648 Treaty of Westphalia.

The key idea that Mann retains from Lattimore is that power networks are not always coterminous. They can be of different sizes. In a multi-ethnic, multireligious empire, military and, to a lesser extent, political networks extend to a much larger territory than either ideological or economic networks. The Austro-Hungarian and Ottoman empires were good examples of that: they possessed a single set of political and military institutions but, apart from these elite *fora*, the various "peoples," differing in language, religion, and level of economic development, were unlikely to come into contact with each other. Conversely, the economy of a city state may depend on its being at the heart of long trading routes even though it is not integrated with its trading partners ideologically, politically, or militarily. That was certainly the case with Amsterdam, Venice, or Genoa: their merchants would have traveled the world and brought back stories to tell their fellow citizens, but this economic interdependence did not entail any sense of common identity with their customers.

The national state, however, can be defined as an almost perfect territorial overlap of the four sources of power. The Western European state made ideological, political, economic, and military networks coincide (Bartolini 2005). Resulting from the interaction of economic and military power relations, the national state "shed its puny historical frame and emerged interstitially—without anyone intending it—as a major authoritative power in its own right" (Mann 1993: 737). In the militarist phase that lasted until the nineteenth century, military and political networks became virtually indistinguishable (Mann 1993: 730). The state came to monopolize means of physical coercion over a given territory. As rulers centralized power, their bureaucracy was able to bound and regulate economic activity, affirming its authority over fiscal revenue, coinage, and trade. The state also domesticated ideological issues (notably religious ones), thus asserting its monopoly over what Bourdieu calls "symbolic violence," or the ability to impose relations of domination through social representations, without the subject even noticing it (Bourdieu 2001).

In other words, the national state became what Anthony Giddens (1987) calls a "bordered power container." Or, as Mann (1993: 251) puts it, "people became trapped within national cages." For most people, the crystallization of ideological, military, economic, and political networks into one coherent, self-enclosed entity (the national state) meant that their *radius* of social interaction had actually expanded. The Royal Mail or *Die Post* allowed one to communicate with distant cousins. The train, often privately run but planned by the state, took one places (Dobbin 1994). Military service forced one to socialize with fellow citizens (Weber 1974). As Karl Deutsch, the father of transactionalism argued, the genesis of the national state, for all its coercive mechanisms, resulted in an expansion and densification of social communication far beyond state institutions. There emerged a national media field, a national sports field, a national public sphere, a national literary field; in other words, a national community.

Deutsch believed that this experience could be replicated on the international level. Describing federal states as *amalgamated* security communities, he thought that an increase in the level and density of communication among elites from different countries could result in the emergence of *pluralistic* security communities, that is, groupings of states characterized by a sense of mutual trust, a common identity ("a sense of we-ness"), and "dependable expectations of peaceful change" (Deutsch et al. 1957; Adler and Barnett 1998). For that to occur, the growth of economic, ideological, and political interaction would force the military to catch up, thus making war and the preparation for war unlikely in the security community. Deutsch sensed that, in the future, economic, ideological, political, and military fields may no longer be so tightly coupled with the national state.[5]

There is a vast literature on the contemporary state that can be more or less summarized as a description of how the four power networks identified by Mann are no longer quite congruent. The literature on globalization suggests that the economic radius of social integration has enlarged in a way that escapes the control of political networks. In other words, we are witnessing the emergence of a global economic field while political

---

[5] For the purposes of this book, a security community in the sense that it is used by Deutsch would not strictly speaking be a field because it unites political entities and not social actors. See Mérand and Pouliot (2008) for a discussion of the links between field and security community.

fields remain more or less bound by the national territory; social fields are decoupled. The expansion of the ideological field is less clear, as instances of "world culture" coexist with the endurance, and sometimes return to, local forms of symbolic attachment (Castells 1996; Strange 1996; Held et al. 1999).

As for military power networks, they are assumed to remain predominantly national. Some authors, like Martin Shaw, argue that the absence of interstate violence within Western Europe, North America, Japan, and Australasia signals of emergence of a global state, a "massive, institutionally complex and messy agglomeration of state power" (Shaw 1997: 501; see also Shaw 2000). David Held (1999) and his colleagues also speak of "military globalization." But most commentators assume that military power remains an attribute of the national state—and is likely to remain so for the foreseeable future. There is, in this view, little room for transnational military solidarity. In the words of Jolyon Howorth (2000*b*: 82), referring to the EU decision-making process, "one cannot send young men to die in a foreign field by qualified majority voting."

Nowhere is the reconfiguration of state power clearer than in the EU. In spite of their differences, students of the EU usually agree that the process of European integration has resulted in a territorial entity that is tightly integrated economically and juridically, much less so ideologically and politically, even less so socially, and not at all militarily. To use Mann's conceptualization of globalization, European firms operate in a transnational-to-global network of social interaction while European citizens, workers, and consumers remain wedded to national networks of interaction (Mann 1997). This seems largely congruent with theories of multilevel governance, which predict that European integration will proceed at different speeds depending on the social field under study (Marks et al. 1996). While the economic field is heavily populated by supranational actors like the Commission and multinational firms, the political field remains predominantly national, albeit with an increasing presence on the part of Brussels institutions like the European Parliament. As Stefano Bartolini (2005) argues, the development of a political system (what he calls "political structuring") somewhat lags behind the concentration of power at the European level (what he calls "centre formation").

There is in fact little research on the extent to which the social field where security and defence actors interact has also become Europeanized. This discussion has been hampered by an understanding of "Brussels" as being the centre of either an international organization or a putative state. For those who adhere to the former view, like Stanley Hoffmann (1995) and his intergovernmentalist followers, the creation of a common economic and legal space will not lead to integration in issues of high politics like security and defence which, because they constitute the core of national sovereignty, cannot willingly be foregone by the state without it losing its *raison d'être*. For those who want to see the EU as a state in the making, like neofunctionalists, security and defence integration could only come about as a spillover from economic, legal, and political unification. These scholars have focused mostly on identifying fields of interaction that are Europeanizing rapidly as a result of supranational economic initiatives, like corporate governance or environmental policy (Haas 1958; Sandholtz and Stone Sweet 1998). Military integration has seemed too tough a test for their predictions.

Our review of political sociological theories of state formation suggests that there is another way of approaching the problem. Without assuming that the future will repeat the past, one can probe the ways in which military integration is emerging *from the interstices* of political, ideological, and economic integration. The European security and defence field that would then be created will not resemble the militarist crystallization of the national state. In fact, the institutionalization of ESDP, in the context of strong economic integration but weak political and ideological integration, suggests that we are witnessing a transformation of the European state, one in which "Dying for the European Union" can begin to make sense. But this new *ultima ratio* will not replace *Pro Patria Mori* because the sources of state power have changed; the purpose of the state has changed; and the symbolic effectiveness of the state has changed.

THEORETICAL FRAMEWORK AND OUTLINE OF THE BOOK

My focus on state transformation thus places ESDP in the historical perspective of European integration. The expansion of diplomatic and military relations within the EU suggests that defence policy, like many other policy arenas, is being denationalized. But that does not mean that the national state has been superseded. In Chapter 1, in what I call the "low politics of high politics," I describe the institutional arrangements and social practices of European defence to show that, empirically, we are in the presence of a *transgovernmental field*, with its own set of actors, rules, social representations, and power structures. Transgovernmentalism is a notion that Wallace and Wallace (2000) use to describe the growing intensity of interaction among EU government actors. In contrast to the "two-level game" model of liberal intergovernmentalism, these relations are not necessarily channeled through "chiefs of government"; rather, they occur at several different levels of the state. As I will show, the density of relations among defence and foreign policymakers around ESDP is indeed striking.

To fully comprehend the implications of what may look like a simple description, a bit of institutional theory is required. A transgovernmental field is a structured and hierarchical social space in which state actors from different countries look to each other, know their place vis-à-vis each other, share and sometimes clash over social representations, and struggle for influence over policy outcomes, domestic and supranational (Powell and DiMaggio 1991; Fligstein 2001*a*). The repetition of patterns of interaction is equivalent to the creation of rules; their stabilization is equivalent to the creation of institutions. Incumbent actors seek to create stable sets of rules because these reinforce their dominant position. Others have no other option than to accept these rules if they want to be part of the game. Over time, all actors come to internalize the power structure and social representations that dominate the field. While national diplomats and military officers remain the main actors of the European security and defence field, it becomes increasingly difficult for them to avoid playing the EU game: to borrow from Bourdieu's terminology, they buy into the *illusio* of the field, they become invested with the sense of the game (Bourdieu 1980, 1997). Once institutionalized, fields thus take a life of their own; their structures constrain social action and escape the control of individual actors—*they become self-sustaining systems*. That is why ESDP, if it does indeed constitute a transgovernmental field as I am arguing here, has made significant progress in recent years and is unlikely to disappear from the EU's agenda.

This begs the question of how fields emerge, of their genesis. Although fields can plausibly be created by fiat, they usually emerge from the interstices of the existing social order, often when that order is "in shock." Periods of institutional stability are punctuated by periods of fluidity. This, I argue, is exactly what happened in the case of ESDP. For reasons that will be detailed below, ways of organizing security and foreign policy cooperation stemming from the conditions of the Cold War were threatened by the demise of the East–West divide. ESDP emerged as an institutional solution to this manifold crisis. To be sure, this solution was pushed by actors with sometimes considerable "social skills," that is, the "ability to engage others in collective action" by bricolaging common frames of meaning (Fligstein 2001*b*). This is what Bourdieu (1997) calls *ars inveniendi*, or the social creativity that comes with knowing the rules of the game. But the "solution" of an ESDP appeared credible to them and other key actors precisely because, while relatively new in form and content, it respected existing power structures and relied on familiar practices and social representations. The successful policy, in turn, forced security and defence actors to come into contact with each other in a structured fashion; the stakes and opportunities for interaction opened up by ESDP resulted in the creation of a new transgovernmental field.

In the perspective adopted here, the past thus weighs heavily on the present. To explain why and how ESDP came about, I look at two distinct processes of institutional integration that unfolded over the past 50 years:

The internationalization of European armed forces since the end of World War II. Thanks to the integrated structures of the Atlantic Alliance and the growth of multinational interventions since the end of the Cold War, West European armed forces increasingly look like multinational corporations: they operate on a global theatre; their manpower is international in outlook; and their governing structures are increasingly similar. *Mutatis mutandis*, they have moved towards small all-volunteer forces (or an all-volunteer core), covering a wide spectrum of tasks, and usually intervening in a multinational context in missions that are only loosely related to "national" defence. To a large extent, this international defence field stabilized around NATO institutions, rules, and social representations. I explore this field in Chapter 2.

The Europeanization of foreign policy since the beginnings of the EU. For the past 50 years, diplomacy in Europe has been mainly about Brussels. The vast majority of European diplomats are involved in shaping the EU's foreign policy or the EU itself, that is, they are involved in the EU's both external and internal dimension. This has created a dense web of relations around EU business, which involves officials working on community (e.g. trade, competition), functional (e.g. United Nations (UN), disarmament), regional (e.g. Middle East, Africa), and institutional (e.g. European Summits) issues. This interaction shaped what I call, in Chapter 3, the European foreign policy field.

European defence is the result of these processes in two ways. First, ESDP would not have been possible without the stock of institutional links and the culture of cooperation that built up, separately, in the defence and foreign policy fields. Without the development of practices of military cooperation within NATO, the cost of an EU role in defence policy would be too exacting. The lack of an infrastructure for military cooperation goes a long way towards explaining the fate of the EDC in the 1950s: one of the main criticisms made by opponents of the EDC was that it was unrealistic, that it was "premature"; in other words, that the cost of transition to a European army would be too high. But without a strong commitment with the EU's foreign policy, ESDP would not have even been contemplated. Because NATO is so strongly associated with the US, only the EU could provide legitimacy to further military integration. The attempt in the mid-1990s to "Europeanize" NATO without involving the EU (the so-called European security and defence identity) bears witness to this.

Second, ESDP is, to a large extent, a new field that is constituted by the overlapping of the international defence and the European foreign policy fields: its mandate, membership, structure, practices, and social representations can be analysed as a mixture, for lack of a better word, of characteristics from NATO and EU foreign policy. As Hanna Ojanen (2006) writes, ESDP can be analysed as the *fusion* of NATO and EU logics.

In these two factors there is a strong element of path dependence (Pierson 1996). Yet while the existence of two fields, the military and the diplomatic, was a necessary condition for ESDP to emerge, it was not a sufficient one. In Chapter 4, I argue that the international defence and the European foreign policy field each underwent crises in the early 1990s. The end of the Cold War and their own fiscal problems led West European governments to slash military spending. Military organizations faced both a budgetary and a legitimacy crisis. This forced them to find ways, beyond traditional defence, to regain legitimacy and salvage their resources. Meanwhile, with the Single European Act and the Treaty of Maastricht, EU policy began to pervade domestic policymaking. The domestication of EU policy meant that foreign ministries were no longer each other's sole interlocutors in the EU. The influence of European diplomats abroad was also called into question in the Balkans, in Africa, and elsewhere. In the early 1990s, Europe was portrayed as an economic giant but a political dwarf.

Chapters 4 and 5 are devoted to explaining how strategic state actors interpreted these crises, and sought to propose different institutional solutions which, to a lesser or greater extent, called for the overlapping of the international defence and European foreign policy fields, and thus the creation of a new, larger field of social interaction. One of these solutions was ESDP, but others were proposed, notably the revitalization of the Western European Union and the European security and defence identity. Taking a closer look at the creation of ESDP, I will highlight the contingent and creative dimension of the "interstitial" formation of a transgovernmental field.

Indeed, one of the contentions of this book is that, from a theoretical point of view, it did not matter much which institutional framework was selected. All institutional options relied on the convergence of defence and foreign policy fields and the coordination of military and diplomatic instruments in the name of the EU. None of the blueprints made a direct connection between a putative federal state and its attendant defence arm. But no one contemplated the possibility that European states would continue to go it alone either.

From the perspective of political sociology, what matters is the willingness on the part of state actors to think beyond national defence, and therefore beyond the categories of the national state. In this sense, as I argue in the concluding chapter, the development of ESDP constitutes a tough but conclusive test to argue the transgovernmentalist case. Some scholars have put forward the claim that the dynamics of governance have shifted towards a regional or even a global order (Slaughter 2004; Katzenstein 2005). The Europeanization of the military implies that the link between defence policy and the national state, which was at the core of state formation for the past five centuries, can no longer be taken for granted. The proposition I put forward in the conclusion is that defence policy is being Europeanized precisely because defence is no longer seen by elites and public opinion as a fundamental part of state identity.

OTHER PERSPECTIVES ON EUROPEAN DEFENCE

The approach I take is quite different from the one adopted in most of the research on ESDP. As Patricia Chilton (1997: 83) remarked, much of the literature on European security is either normatively driven or policy oriented. In the normative category one finds the writings of a number of government officials, political theorists, and commentators concerned with the role the EU should play on the world stage. There is, for example, an enduring debate on whether the EU should acquire a military dimension (*Europe puissance*) or focus instead on civilian tasks (Europe as a civilian or normative power).[6] In the policy category one finds foreign policy experts, who often work in think tanks, advise governments, and write op-ed columns on issues such as the impact of ESDP on transatlantic relations, military capability, and crisis management.[7]

The two founding fathers of EU studies had very little to say about security and defence cooperation. For Ernst Haas, the neofunctionalist, European integration was bound to unfold relatively smoothly. Beginning in narrow policy domains, functional integration would spill over onto an ever increasing number of policy domains. For example, the integration of coal and steel industries would force states to contemplate the integration of affected domains such as energy policy and labour relations. As bits of sovereignty were incrementally pooled in Brussels, interest groups would be attracted to the emerging political system, thus slowly shifting their loyalty to a new centre. The process of *engrenage* meant that domestic actors would see that their fates were increasingly shaped in Brussels, thus preventing renationalization. But in *The Uniting of Europe*, Haas focused on economic, legal, and regulatory domains. Writing in 1958, after the failure of the EDC, Haas did not venture to make predictions about whether functional integration would spill over onto security and

---

[6] Arguments in favour of *Europe puissance* are found in Bull (1982); Gnesotto (1998); Patten (2001); and Cooper (2004). Arguments in favour of civilian or normative power are found in Duchêne (1972); Balibar (2003); Todorov (2003); Leonard (2005); Telò (2005); and Manners (2006).

[7] The names of François Heisbourg, Nicole Gnesotto, and Gilles Andréani in France; Christoph Bertram and Karl Lamers in Germany; Julian Lindley-French, Michael Quinlan, Paul Cornish, and Charles Grant in the UK; or Philip Gordon, Stanley Sloan, and Robert Hunter in the US come to mind.

defence policy, at least not so long as a European *demos* did not come into existence—a rather distant prospect, even today. His contemporary, Karl Deutsch, did write about the prospects of defence cooperation and identity formation, which he thought would be ushered in by the creation of security communities, but he had in mind the Atlantic Alliance, not the EU. As of today, few authors have dared to apply the concept of spillover or security community to European security and defence cooperation.[8]

A few years after the publication of Haas's book, Stanley Hoffmann (1966) used the empirical absence of defence cooperation, exemplified by the failure of the EDC, to illustrate what he saw as the theoretical limits of European integration. In Hoffmann's version of intergovernmentalism, the state is more obstinate than obsolete. States can resign themselves to share sovereignty when their "national situation" meets favourable conditions. But inevitably, functional integration will reach an end when it approaches the core of the national sovereignty, what he called "high politics" and the French call "politique régalienne": defence, diplomacy, and currency. For Hoffmann, sovereignty is like an artichoke: the leaves are easier to swallow than the heart (gourmets may dispute this).

In a recent article, Hanna Ojanen (2006) makes a brave attempt at applying neofunctionalism and intergovernmentalism to the creation of ESDP. But she shows that their predictions for ESDP are indeterminate. Both approaches can be invoked to argue that security and defence cooperation is *either* impossible *or* inevitable. On the one hand, the Europeanization of defence policy is impossible in the absence of a European *demos*, which is a prerequisite for the functioning of a European political system. Without a *demos*, it cannot be said that a transfer of loyalty at the transnational level has completely occurred (what Haas calls the "takeoff effect") or that the locus of sovereignty upon which Hoffmann's analysis is based has been displaced. On the other hand, the success of functional integration cannot leave defence policy aside forever; there are huge economies of scale to be made in the area of defence policy, which only Europeanization can bring about. Thus, the theories of Haas and Hoffmann can be called upon to argue both for *and* against European defence cooperation. Given this theoretical indeterminacy, it is not surprising that a "transtheoretical consensus on the specificity of security and defence policy" has inhibited

---

[8] One partial exception is Collester (2001).

contemporary neofunctionalist and intergovernmentalist scholars from studying ESDP (Ojanen 2006: 60).

With a few exceptions, contemporary scholars who have tackled ESDP are more in tune with the canons of International Relations (IR) theory than with the two classical paradigms of EU studies. In particular, neorealism, liberalism, constructivism, and foreign policy analysis have enjoyed considerable currency. I now turn to a discussion of each.

Neorealism

Most authors have stuck to the orthodox notion that governments remain in full control of security and defence policy. The idea here is that ESDP is yet another play of power politics. States are homogenous, unitary actors that seek to protect their sovereignty and expand their influence. In contrast to Hoffmann's artichoke metaphor, this assumption holds for all policy domains. Naturally, the capacity to protect one's sovereignty is conditional upon state strength. Unless it is framed in a way that empowers the major states at the expense of smaller ones, European defence is doomed to fail. That is why ESDP is largely driven by the three biggest military powers, the UK, France, and to a lesser extent Germany. These countries are instrumentalizing Europe to attain broader strategic objectives, especially vis-à-vis the US. "From a realist perspective," writes Hyde-Price (2006: 222), "EU external policy cooperation constitutes a collective attempt at milieu shaping [seeking stability], driven primarily by the Union's largest powers." These large powers are constrained only by the nature of the international system: "Two developments were crucial to the ESDP initiative: the preponderance of US power globally (unipolarity) and balanced multipolarity in Europe" (Hyde-Price 2006: 228). More specifically, the UK and France have embarked on ESDP "to enhance their political influence within the transatlantic alliance through soft balancing, but not to challenge America's military hegemony with hard balancing" (Art 2004: 199). Barry Posen (2004, 2006) also advances a "weak balance-of-power" argument, but makes room for the possibility that Europeans, fed up with US unilateralism, may one day seek further military autonomy.

The neorealist framework has been used explicitly to make a link between power politics and the EU's military intervention in the Congo, which has been analysed more or less as a French plot (Gegout 2005). In the most exhaustive neorealist account of ESDP so far, which borrows a great deal from the arguments made by Mearsheimer, Art, and Posen, Seth Jones argues that two structural shifts in the international and European systems have led to a substantial increase in European security cooperation. The withdrawal of the US from Europe after the end of the Cold War created a power vacuum in which it became possible for big European states to pursue their dream of strategic autonomy. In parallel, France and Britain "adopted a *binding* strategy...to tie Germany into Europe and increase the likelihood of peace on the continent" (Jones 2007: 11). This binding strategy, which Jones contrasts with bandwagoning and balancing, was made possible because Germany is a status quo power. Looking at economic sanctions (CFSP), weapons production, and military forces (ESDP), Jones finds that London, Paris, and Berlin have been the predominant actors in the field of European security; his interpretation is that ESDP is essentially part of a broader strategy to increase their power, both vis-à-vis each other and vis-à-vis Washington.

While neorealist approaches to ESDP are only beginning to appear in print, the pervasiveness of neorealist assumptions is often implicit. The subtext of most available analyses is that ESDP is a circumstantial compromise between states trying strategically to further their interest. Britain and France in particular are pursuing ulterior motives: namely, to strengthen its leadership among EU states for the former, and to multiply its declining world influence through Europe for the latter. Germany simply wishes to free ride by supporting as many security arrangements as possible (Calleo 2001; Treacher 2001, 2004; Eilstrup-Sangiovanni 2003). My approach differs from this perspective in three ways. First, although I agree that *representatives* from heavyweight states have more political capital and therefore influence, I do not consider "states" to be meaningful, purposive actors. Although I will often use the names of countries or capital cities as shorthand, to say that a "state wants something" makes no ontological sense. Second, occasional Gaullist rhetoric notwithstanding, there is little evidence that European leaders from the UK or France try to balance the US, much less tie Germany to their domination. This *ex post* rationalization is not borne out by any of the interviews I conducted.

It may have applied to the EDC (Eilstrup-Sangiovanni and Verdier 2005) but not to ESDP, which neorealists seem to construe as a simple continuation of the failed French project. Finally, as will become clear in the demonstration, I attribute relatively little importance to the role of Washington in launching ESDP: from my perspective, important actors were Europeans and the process of institutionalization was internal to Europe.

Liberalism

The state interest-centred subtext also comes out among scholars of a more liberal sensibility who, like Andrew Moravcsik (2003: 83), argue that ESDP is a "pipe dream." It is at best a form of power laundering for European states that have grown wary of being portrayed as neocolonial and find it useful to use a European fig leaf. But this rhetorical strategy carries the risk of alienating Washington. Rather than wasting resources and time on military grandstanding, the EU should focus on its "functional specificity," namely, civilian crisis management and foreign trade. For liberals, states should never lose sight of their self-interest, but they sometimes realize that certain multilateral arrangements that overcome coordination problems can help them reach their selfish goals. That is why NATO exists, which EU member states, if they are rational, should not try to duplicate. NATO was institutionalized in the specific historical context of a Euro-Atlantic military and economic alliance against the Soviet Union. It now offers a US security guarantee to European states that allows them to focus on economic and trade issues (Wallander, Haftendorn, and Keohane 1999).

European defence has very little future because issue areas pertaining to high politics can be integrated only with great difficulty. ESDP, in this view, is hampered by a deep-seated conflict of interests between member states: beyond time-wasting declaratory diplomacy and gestures of goodwill, each state follows its own strategic interest at the lowest cost possible. Economically, they have little to gain and too much to lose from getting involved in an ambitious defence project that competes with the US-backed Atlantic Alliance.

The problem, of course, is that Europeans *are* doing it, and that this begs for an explanation. I take issue with liberal approaches to military cooperation (bearing in mind that there are very few) because they tend to grant causal primacy to economic interests or business groups, both of which seem to have played a minor role in the development of ESDP, except in providing *one* of the rationales for military integration. This may change, however, with the development of a competitive European defence industry eager to play a policy role in Brussels (Mörth 2004). Hopefully this will allow liberals to expand their research program.

Constructivism

Constructivism emerged in the 1980s as a way to revive idealist theories of the international system and against the hegemony of the so-called "rationalist" theories, such as neorealism and liberalism, which attribute consequentiality to states. To do so, an attempt was made to conceptualize the influence of norms, ideas, discourses, identities, all of which suggest that states follow a logic of appropriateness (Finnemore 1996). For constructivists, ESDP is part of a broader context in which security actors "coordinate their action through deliberation and argument" in an increasing number of European forums, such as the Organization for Security and Cooperation in Europe (OSCE), the Council of Europe, or the EU (Checkel 2005; Sjursen 2006). The debate on European defence is an element of the EU's international identity and, as such, it exhibits the communicative and symbolic characteristics of the European project.

Besides a policy, ESDP is a discourse. Jolyon Howorth (2003) tries to make this approach more concrete in an article where he argues that, since the beginning, ESDP suffered from London's inability to produce a coherent communicative discourse about its intentions. This, for Howorth, is particularly important because ESDP was created by an "epistemic community" of policymakers, based in the French and British foreign and defence ministries, whose main challenge was to work out a common vocabulary for European security.

As a neorealist critic of constructivism points out, the EU cannot be expected to forge a common defence policy on the basis of disparate strategic cultures (Rynning 2003). Constructivists have thus paid a great deal of attention to the question of whether strategic norms and beliefs are converging in the EU. Bastian Giegerich (2006) proposes a sober assessment by documenting the enduring diversity of strategic cultures among EU states. Christoph Meyer (2006), however, argues that there has been a certain degree of convergence since 1989 around threat perceptions, and that this convergence is attributable to new forms of cross-socialization. This cross-socialization can be observed, he argues, in Brussels-based institutions such as the Political and Security Committee (COPS), where "security and defence" ambassadors meet once a week, and the EU Military Committee. Cultural convergence is also driven by common learning from the crises that plagued the European continent in the 1990s, notably the Balkan wars.

Thanks to these experiences, France was able to embrace a NATO-friendly project like ESDP because the Gaullist legacy, which had stressed strategic autonomy from the Alliance, subsided. Germany switched from a culture of reticence based on soft security and NATO primacy to a more interventionist stance. Britain, finally, began to understand that its fate lay on the European continent, and that the "special relationship" with Washington needed to be supplemented with a stronger European identity.

In sum, for constructivists, the question is whether state identities will be redirected in a way that stresses their community of fate (Anderson and Seitz 2006). The ultimate guarantee of a successful ESDP is the consolidation of a European strategic culture. The existence of such a culture relies on a process of "group formation" (Tonra 2003). "The critical question, writes Anthony King (2005: 48), is whether Britain, France and Germany can create sufficiently dense social relations so that their collective interests converge further and they are mutually able to enjoin each other to address them. There is some evidence, he adds, that these member states are beginning to orient themselves consciously to collective goals."

Constructivists are famously unclear about who the carriers of this strategic culture are. Although King concedes that a strategic culture can only emerge through "missions which unify military professionals and consolidate collective interests in a way which mere statements of policy never can," thus acknowledging the importance of actors, he cannot resist the temptation to say that *states* behave "consciously" (King 2005: 57). In my view, the reification of the "state," its "identity," and its "culture" constitutes an important shortcoming of many constructivist approaches. At the end of the day, they, like neorealists, tend to treat the state as a single unit with a coherent identity. This makes the approach underdetermining.

It does little to explain why governments sometimes change course: identities and culture are not known to be prone to change. Nor does constructivism help us to understand why governments sometimes pursue policies that are at odds with their public, which implies that countries have split "identities." More importantly, constructivism does not make allowance for the fact that perceptions of European defence are not consistent or homogenous. In each country, with some variation, some support ESDP while others do not. ESDP, like other policies, is the object of struggles. This suggests that states can hardly be treated as single units that enact identities.

Foreign Policy Analysis

What I call the fourth approach is more like a basket case of different theoretical frameworks that share an emphasis on the role of *domestic* political and bureaucratic *actors*. I subsume these frameworks under the heading of "foreign policy analysis," fully cognizant of the fact that some of the authors discussed here would probably refer to their work as being part of the "decision-making" or "bureaucratic politics" traditions.

The strength of foreign policy analysis is to try and instill some analytical rigour in narrative accounts that could otherwise be characterized as diplomatic history. A great deal of writing on ESDP reads like personal diaries of the political leaders who carried out ESDP negotiations. There is a bias towards accepting political actors' justifications at face value. Foreign policy analysts, however, try to go beyond the proximate causes of the European defence project by embedding them in the broader context of action. They relax the assumption that only heads of government matter and try to map out the institutional conditions underpinning the decision-making process (White 2001). In particular, foreign policy analysis looks at the key bureaucratic and political actors, the capabilities and instruments they have at their disposal, the rules and dynamics of the foreign policy process, and the opportunities and constraints of the broader policy environment wherein decision-making takes place.

In France, Bastien Irondelle (2003a) has shown that Europeanization was a conscious strategy on the part of decision-makers to transform the cognitive and institutional structures of French defence policy. This "Europeanization without the European Union" began to take place long before ESDP was launched, in the early 1990s. In Britain, Robert Dover (2005) documents how the European Defence Initiative emerged in the context of tense policy discussions among Cabinet members and officials from the Foreign Office, the Ministry of Defence, and the Defence Staff. He thus complements Rathbun's (2004) argument that British partisan politics mattered: the coming to power of a Labour government in 1997 created the political space for British officials to launch an initiative that was hitherto considered anathema. In Sweden, Arita Eriksson (2006) has proposed a detailed account of the adaptation of defence policymakers to the European mode of governance.

At the EU level, Duke and Ojanen (2006) have explored the bureaucratic rivalries that plague ESDP. The EU Council, the Commission, the Franco-British-German *directoire*, and member states in general can all claim to have some competence over ESDP, but each has its own agenda. By linking up domestic and supranational decision-making frameworks, this analytical lens opens up a broad research agenda on the fragmented governance of European security, where conflicting demands for effectiveness and legitimacy become increasingly salient (Webber et al. 2004; Giegerich and Gross 2006).

What is missing from these important theoretical contributions, however, is a long-term perspective on the genesis of ESDP. Too often this literature emphasizes *ex post* analytic descriptions of particular decision-making contexts at the expense of theoretical explanation. In particular, foreign policy analysis lacks a theory of why bureaucratic and political actors behave the way they do; how they translate their positions into actions; and most importantly which social mechanisms, both short and long term, explain the outcome of the policy process. By contrast, the argument I make in this book is that ESDP would not exist had it not been built on 50 years of defence and foreign policy cooperation, a framework that was threatened after 1989. A focus on strategic decisions, communicative processes, or policymaking *stricto sensu* cannot fully explain why state actors are *able* and *willing* to work towards the establishment of a common defence policy. Furthermore, the defence and foreign policy fields that were institutionalized since the 1940s shape the emerging ESDP field to a very large extent. Their membership, structures, practices, and social representations go a long way towards explaining the functioning of ESDP.

This book is also an attempt at embedding ESDP in a broader political sociology argument about state transformation in Europe. The creation of a regional defence policy is unimaginable in any other part of the world. We may be witnessing the coming of a "world of regions," but none of these regions has been associated with the transformation of the states within them that makes government actors likely to consider relinquishing the traditional attributes of state sovereignty (Katzenstein 2005). Only in Europe is it possible to imagine that one would die for what many academics continue to see as a trading bloc.

1

What is European Defence?

On 30 August 1954, the French National Assembly dealt a lethal blow to the project of EDC. The EDC, agreed upon by the six founding members of the ECSC in Paris two years before, would have been composed of multinational combat teams, with a common budget and under the authority of a European defence minister. The historical significance of the EDC was not lost on contemporaries; had it been ratified, the Treaty of Paris would have led to what friends and foes called the "European army."

There are many reasons why the EDC failed to convince French deputies. One of them, foreseen by Winston Churchill who called it a "sludgy amalgam," was its top–down character. Looking over a long-term horizon of European unification, Jean Monnet, the inventor of the Coal and Steel Community, and René Pleven, the French Prime Minister in 1952, had designed a very supranational project that few French politicians could stomach less than 10 years after the end of World War II. When the treaty came for ratification, it was blocked by a slim majority dominated by Gaullists and Communists. Also, bogged down in Indochina and with armed forces that they were just beginning to rebuild, the military establishment could not see how to translate this grand political design into a credible military structure (Aron and Lerner 1956; Parsons 2004). The failure of the EDC led Stanley Hoffmann (1966) to argue that, in the high politics of foreign and defence policy, European integration would remain but a chimera.

When, at the December 1998 St. Malo Summit, Jacques Chirac and Tony Blair launched the European Defence Initiative, many believed it would meet the same fate as the EDC. Yet, over the following years, ESDP made remarkable progress. In less time than it took to forge the Economic and Monetary Union, the EU established a Political and Security Committee, a Military Committee, a Military Staff, a Defence Agency, and EU Battle Groups. Military operations were undertaken in Macedonia, the Congo, and Bosnia. In the ill-fated Constitutional Treaty, EU leaders even agreed to a "solidarity clause" that is only one step short of NATO's mutual defence clause, Article 5. The EU's solidarity clause specifies that EU member states can come to each other's assistance in case of a terrorist attack or any natural disaster, while the Alliance's Article 5 is automatic and includes any armed attack.

To a large extent, the success of ESDP can be attributed to its bottom–up approach. Avoiding the pitfalls of a political discussion on the *finalité* of European defence, officials focused their minds on modest forms of cooperation, small organizational structures, and relatively safe military operations. The theological quibbles of EDC gave way to cautious, pragmatic incrementalism. Symbolically, however, European defence does remain pregnant with meaning. Already envisaged in the 1950s as a means to make war impossible between France and Germany, protect the West against the Soviet bloc, and give Europe an autonomous voice in international affairs, European defence is a powerful illustration of what a "political Europe" with global ambitions could one day become. Remarkably, it is one of the most popular EU initiatives among European publics (Manigart 2001). Thus, the fundamental achievements of ESDP are not to be found in its institutional design but in its political–practical implications: tightening forms of military cooperation; converging social representations about the role of armed forces; the nature of threats and ways to address them; and, more importantly perhaps, an explicit willingness to integrate further (or at least not go backwards) in the near future. This is what Howorth (2007) has called "co-odigration" and what I call a "transgovernmental field."

Taking European defence as a "social fact," to use Emile Durkheim's dictum, rather than as a simple policy instrument, this chapter describes European defence as a set of concrete institutions and tangible social practices that bring together foreign and defence actors from EU member states. It is very consciously that I eschew diplomatic commentary and strategic considerations and focus instead on the "low politics" of high politics.

ESDP

On the face of it, ESDP is not a policy, and it has little to do with defence. Enshrined in the 2001 Treaty of Nice, it is first and foremost a decision-making structure that enables the EU to launch crisis management operations and pursue its foreign policy objectives. At some point in 2001 there were slightly fewer than 10,000 peacekeepers deployed under EU command across the globe. Since 2003, the EU flag has adorned military and police uniforms in Bosnia, Macedonia, Palestine, Sudan, the Democratic Republic of Congo, and Chad, in addition to several more modest civilian crisis management operations. Notwithstanding the shortcomings of ESDP, what seemed like a distant prospect at the turn of the century is now a reality, with concrete implications for European foreign and defence policy actors.

Crisis Management Operations

The first EU police operation was launched in January 2003 in Bosnia-Herzegovina. A few months later, the EU deployed its first *military* operation in Macedonia, with 400 uniformed personnel. Operation Concordia, whose purpose was to implement the Ohrid Framework Agreement between Macedonian Slavs and Albanians, took over from NATO but, under the so-called Berlin Plus Agreement, relied extensively on the assets and capabilities of the Atlantic Alliance. This means that, while the mission was under the political authority of European diplomats and staffed by European soldiers, the planning and conduct of the operation were located in NATO headquarters. This operation was followed by a police mission, Proxima, also conducted by the EU.

In a matter of weeks, the EU launched its first "autonomous" military operation in Bunia, capital of the eastern Congolese region of Ituri. The aim of the operation was to protect internally displaced persons and civilians, secure the Bunia airport, and assist the bigger UN mission (MONUC) (Bagayoko 2005*a*; Gegout 2005). Although mainly staffed by the French, the 2,000-strong Operation Artemis was widely seen as a landmark because it was conducted without recourse to NATO assets and capabilities (hence the term "autonomous"). The troops were overwhelmingly European, as were the chain of command and capabilities.

These relatively safe operations gave credibility to what had so far amounted to little more than an organization chart. The December 2002 European Council had stated that the EU would be willing to take on an even bigger mission than these two, namely the peace support operation carried out by NATO in Bosnia since the signing of the Dayton agreements in 1995. This became a real possibility in June 2004 when, at the Istanbul Summit, NATO agreed to terminate SFOR and pass the baton to the EU. Operation Althea, a 7,000-strong EU Force that also relies on NATO assets and capabilities, was launched on 2 December of that year. With Bosnia, the EU can now claim that it has lots of boots on the ground.

As the EU was preparing to send 2,000 fresh troops to the Democratic Republic of Congo, with a mandate to support MONUC during the July 2006 elections, it was still involved in one other military operation (Althea in Bosnia), one civilian–military support mission (EU Support to the African Union (AU) Mission in Sudan II), three police missions (EUPM in Bosnia, EUPOL COPPS in Palestine, and EUPOL Kinshasa), one security sector reform mission in the Congo, one monitoring mission in Banda Aceh, one rule-of-law mission in Iraq, and two border assistance missions (in Palestine and Moldova). The military operations in Macedonia and the Congo, the police operation in Macedonia, and the rule-of-law mission in Georgia had been completed. In 2007, a police training mission was deployed to Afghanistan. A military operation was about to be launched in Chad, with a mandate to help the UN protect refugees from Darfur.

Between 2003 and 2007, then, 18 crisis management operations were launched by the EU under the ESDP label—ranging from legal advice by a dozen civilian experts to peace enforcement by hundreds of heavily armed soldiers. While ESDP appears modest in comparison to NATO, which remains the most credible multinational alliance, its strength lies in a specific crisis management philosophy, which brings together military and civilian instruments in a toolbox of capabilities that the EU can coordinate and deploy to prevent conflicts, manage crises, and support long-term peace and security in troubled spots around the world (Biscop 2005). By combining substantial development funds, professional expertise, political influence, and decent expeditionary forces, the EU hopes that it can achieve a range of tasks that neither NATO nor the UN (let alone individual states) can undertake on their own (Andréani, Bertram, and Grant 2001: 44). In so doing, Brussels also hopes that it can bolster its emerging foreign policy and become a leading international actor.

In this book, I barely touch upon the civilian aspects of crisis management, illustrated by police and rule-of-law missions (Merlingen and Ostrauskaite 2006). I deal only with the dimension of ESDP that is associated with its primary mandate, the so-called "Petersberg tasks," named after the German castle where European governments met in 1992 to elaborate a strategic concept for the now defunct WEU. These tasks include humanitarian and rescue operations, peacekeeping, and combat force in crisis management, including peacemaking. These kinds of operation must be conducted under a UN mandate. They will usually correspond to the UN Charter's Chapter VI (peacekeeping missions) and Chapter VII (threats to international security). The *military* aspects of ESDP, illustrated by the EU Force in Bosnia and Operation Artemis in the Congo, are, in my view, the most consequential for a study of state transformation in Europe because they constitute the core of our definition of sovereignty.

Political–Military Bodies

Before the EU became a major actor in the deployment of expeditionary forces for peace support operations, much time was expended on the creation of institutions—to the chagrin of the UK government, which wanted the EU to focus on capabilities. This involved primarily the establishment of a number of political–military bodies in the Council of Ministers, the intergovernmental institution of the EU.

The COPS was created in 2000 to ensure the political control and strategic direction of ESDP. Composed of ambassador-level delegates from each of the member states and paralleling NATO's North Atlantic Council, the COPS is the heart of the EU's decision-making process in the area of crisis management (Meyer 2006). Permanently based in Brussels, its members meet at least once a week and have quickly taken over most security files from the old Political Committee, through which political directors used to meet, much less frequently, to discuss issues pertaining to the common foreign and security policy.

The COPS has quickly established itself as one of the EU's most prestigious bodies. Functioning like the General Affairs and External Relations Council on the unanimity principle, it has strengthened the intergovernmental character of EU foreign policy, albeit with a strongly European twist which contrasts with the way foreign policy used to be done between EU capitals. The COPS has become an influential institution both in Brussels and in the capitals precisely because it engages senior national diplomats in an EU context. As a former Council official writes:

The theory is that the Political and Security Committee, meeting frequently, and the Council, meeting once a month, share information and assessments, discuss options, take decisions and ensure implementation. But this is not what really happens. The wheels spin in Brussels, discussions take place in the [COPS] and conclusions are reached by the Council to provide the appearance of policy formulation and implementation. But what makes the EU an effective foreign policy actor..., that is, one influencing outcomes and taken seriously by other players, is not what the [COPS] discusses or thinks; it is, rather, the willingness and ability of a senior individual to get stuck in on its behalf, in close contact with other key players..., with a rather light rein from Brussels (Crowe 2003: 541).

The COPS relies on the military advice and coordination functions of the Military Committee (EUMC). The Military Committee consists of Military Representatives delegated by the member states' Chiefs of Defence Staff and usually double-hatted to sit on NATO's own military committee. They manage military exercises; prepare the plans and concepts of EU crisis management operations; and supervise EU-appointed military commanders. The symbolic importance of the EUMC can hardly be overstated: it has allowed high-ranked military officers, for the first time, to meet and work on EU premises. At the time of its creation, in 2000, this was praised as nothing short of Europe's "military revolution" (Andréani, Bertram, and Grant 2001). The Military Committee required a complete reorganization of the Council Secretariat, notably the securitization of communications and facilities, and forced each member state's Permanent Representation to create about a dozen defence positions in Brussels, up to the rank of general. A Political–Military Group was also set up that brings together EU diplomats and military officers. This has created direct links between European institutions and national military establishments. The increasing number of meetings held in EU Council buildings has led to what insiders call a "Brusselsization" of defence policy, with the result that, today, one can argue that defence staffs have taken ownership of the EU. They were one of the last domestic state institutions to do so but caught up very quickly.

A Military Staff (EUMS) was also established to provide early warning, situation assessment, and strategic planning, supervise force planning procedures, and implement the decision of the Military Committee. It is a directorate-general of the Council Secretariat and, as such, the "only permanent integrated military structure of the EU." Initially envisaged as a modest planning staff to liaise with multinational and national headquarters, the EUMS became something more ambitious after Britain, France, and Germany agreed, in September 2003, to set up a planning cell for autonomous EU operations in the Council Secretariat, in addition to an EU Cell in Supreme Headquarters Allied Powers, Europe (SHAPE), the Allied European headquarters. Today, the Military Staff comprises more than 250 military officers and houses the infrastructure of a small operations headquarters. There are six divisions dealing with planning, intelligence, operations/exercises, logistics, information systems, and civilian–military coordination.

These three political–military bodies are ultimately under the authority of the General Affairs Council, the top intergovernmental decision-making institution in the EU. This "foreign affairs" formation of the Council of Ministers is assisted by a Secretary General, Javier Solana, who is also the EU High Representative for the CFSP and Chairman of the European Defence Agency (EDA) Steering Board. I will go back to the latter in the next section.

The High Representative position was created in 1997 during the negotiations that led to the Treaty of Amsterdam. Championed by Paris as a political figure to help broker agreements among EU governments and give the EU a face in the world, "Mr. CFSP" was eventually agreed by the new Blair government as a way to fend off the European Commission's increasing assertiveness in external relations. The British always had reservations about the post and would have preferred to grant it to a civil servant. But the French and the Germans feared that this would dilute the function. A compromise was found when Javier Solana was appointed in 1999. As a former Socialist minister in Spain and incumbent NATO Secretary

General, the new High Representative "met the French criterion for seniority and proactivism, the British criterion for user-friendly Atlanticism, and the German criterion for Europeanism" (Howorth 2001: 771).

By all accounts, Solana proved to be a consummate political entrepreneur. On paper, his role is merely that of a facilitator and a spokesperson with little room for personal initiative. But thanks to his previous job in NATO and public exposure during the Kosovo War, Solana came to the post with a great deal of political capital (Buchet de Neuilly 2005). He quickly asserted his prerogatives as the "EU's foreign policy chief"—an expression coined by the British press. He became a key interlocutor for countries like the US, in the Middle East, and during EU–Iran nuclear discussions. He also had a major impact on the organization of ESDP structures, bolstering the Policy Unit, creating an ESDP task force, and surrounding himself with a group of influential advisers like Robert Cooper, a former British senior diplomat. As a result of this institutional success, Solana emerged as the most likely candidate for the new position of EU Foreign Minister that the Constitutional Treaty was supposed to create.[1]

Military Capabilities

The fourth political–military body associated with ESDP is the European Defence Agency, created in 2004 to streamline procurement programmes and promote the development of military capabilities. The EDA is an agency with its own steering board made up of EU defence ministers, but chaired by the High Representative. One important characteristic of the EDA is that it is the only political–military body, certainly in the EU but also probably in the world, to make decisions by qualified majority voting (QMV). Bringing together civilian officials, defence staffs, and procurement directors, the EDA is the tentative response to an extremely fragmented defence equipment market characterized by protectionist policies, small national firms, and low levels of investment. Although purchase orders will remain under the purview of national governments, the EDA tries to rationalize the military tools of EU member states by encouraging armaments cooperation, common procurement programs, strategic

---

[1] The 2007 reform treaty will create the post but, following British demands, will retain the somewhat less glamorous title of "High Representative."

research and development, and more generally the Europeanization of the defence sector. In the summer of 2006, the EDA convinced EU governments to adhere to a code of conduct that goes some way towards opening up the defence equipment market. More than €10 billion worth of contract opportunities have already been opened up to competition through the EDA's Bulletin Board.

The EDA is only the last of a long series of initiatives to stimulate armaments cooperation in Europe. Until the 1990s, European projects were usually bilateral and, with a few exceptions, rarely successful. In the 1980s, for example, French firms produced 96% of the French army's equipment (Moravcsik 1993; Gautier 1999: 345–52). Through Article 223 of the Treaty of Rome (Art 296 in the new numbering introduced by the Amsterdam Treaty), armaments were specifically excluded from trade liberalization. It was argued that the defence industry was a matter of national security and that, therefore, Common Market rules were unenforceable. Consultative arrangements between procurement directors in NATO or the WEU had little or no impact (Jones 2007).

Things started to change in 1996, when France, Germany, the UK, and Italy established the *Organisation conjointe de coopération en matière d'armements* (OCCAR). In order to "create a clearly defined set of procedures for managing common programmes," OCCAR members agreed to be more flexible on the "juste retour" principle, which traditionally allows national governments to require that 100% of their purchase share be spent domestically (Keohane 2002: 24; Mörth 2004). Two years later, the same countries (plus Sweden and Spain) signed an important Letter of Intent (LoI) aimed at harmonizing regulation with regards to supply requirements, export procedures, information security, and property rights in the defence procurement sector.

The EDA is an attempt to formalize this patchy set of initiatives in a specifically EU context and with the collaboration of the European Commission, whose Internal Market officials have long tried to limit the scope of Article 296. This is coming at a time when some sectors of the defence industry, notably aerospace with EADS and defence electronics with Thales, are starting to reorganize on a European-wide basis through cross-border mergers and acquisitions (Schmitt 2000). Although this book does not deal with the defence industry, it should be borne in mind that this industry has undergone an unprecedented wave of Europeanization in the past 10 years, leading, around EADS, Thales, BAE Systems, and Finmeccanica, to a highly concentrated sector characterized by cross-ownership structures and joint ventures.

In addition to dealing with technical and market access issues, that is, spending public money *better*, the EDA is supposed to encourage EU governments to spend *more* on military capabilities. At the 1999 Helsinki Summit, EU states decided to set up a rapid reaction force for the nascent ESDP. To put this force in place, they agreed on a Headline Goal, which specified the number of troops and capabilities required: ~60,000 with appropriate air and naval elements. In order to define national contributions, a Capabilities Commitment Conference was held in 2000. It had been known since the early 1990s that Europe lacked the capabilities required for a rapid reaction force, which is why, the following year, a Capabilities Improvement Conference was convened. Defence ministers agreed to put together a European Capabilities Action Plan (ECAP), more or less in line with NATO's own Defence Capabilities Initiative (DCI) and Prague Capabilities Commitment. For that purpose, several European working groups were created, which have now been absorbed into the EDA. As EDA officials acknowledge, one of their biggest challenges consists of supporting national defence staffs in their demands for more spending, but also fewer political considerations in its allocation.[2]

European Forces

The EU does not "own" military capabilities. There are no European armed forces in which national chains of command would be overruled. Only the common costs associated with running the EUMS and maintaining force headquarters on a theatre of operation are shared; other than that, "costs lie where they fall," which means that contributors pay for their own troops and equipment (Missiroli 2003; Schmitt 2003). When the EU decides to launch a mission, it has to mandate SHAPE or a national operations headquarters, such as Britain's Permanent Joint Headquarters (PJHQ) in Northwood, France's *Centre de planification et de conduite des opérations* (CPCO) near Paris, or Germany's *Einsatzführungskommando* in Potsdam, to carry out the operation. For example, Operation Althea in Bosnia was

---

[2] Interview with the author, European Defence Agency, Brussels, 2005.

commanded by General John Reid, Deputy Commander of Allied forces in Europe. Through SHAPE, NATO provides most of the planning for the operation, which includes some troops from non-EU countries, like Canada, Morocco, and Switzerland. This is an example of a Berlin Plus operation, which has recourse to NATO assets and capabilities. Operation Artemis, on the other hand, was an "autonomous" operation, commanded from the French CPCO, augmented by liaison officers from participating countries. France, as the "framework nation," contributed most of the personnel, with some additional staff from the UK, Germany, Sweden, and Belgium. The 2006 operation in the Congo was led by Germany's brand new operations headquarters in Potsdam, which was specifically designed to accommodate a large number of foreign officers.[3]

But the chain of command, instead of leading up to the North Atlantic Council or a member-state's government, is placed under the authority of the EU Council. In other words, soldiers wear an EU badge and risk their lives for EU foreign policy objectives. An EU operation is launched, controlled, and disbanded by the EU. This symbolic dimension will be strengthened with the creation of EU Battle Groups, 1,500-strong joint units that should become the vanguard of autonomous EU operations. Attached to national force headquarters, most of the 15 Battle Groups will be multinational. Infantrymen and support staff from different EU countries will regularly train together and deploy under the same rules of engagement and the same command structure (Andersson 2006). A number of European assets are also being put in place, such as the European Airlift Centre, managed from High Wycombe, UK, by 25-odd military officers from seven European countries. While combined (i.e. multinational) military forces have become almost commonplace since the end of the Cold War, European militaries had not considered the establishment of multinational force packages that would be integrated at a low level and on a permanent basis since the failed EDC.

In deciding which forces to deploy for an ESDP operation, the EU has access to a force catalogue. Designed after the Helsinki Summit to fulfill the needs of the European rapid reaction force, the force catalogue lists national capabilities that can be made available to the EU upon request. In practice, these capabilities are often also assigned to NATO's Response

---

[3] Interview, Bundesministerium der Verteidigung, Berlin, 2002.

Force, which has made many experts wonder how credible these commitments really are (Lindley-French 2002).

The catalogue also includes a number of "European" forces, like the Eurocorps, the European Rapid Operational Force (EUROFOR), and the European Maritime Force (EUROMARFOR), which were created before ESDP to be answerable to the now-defunct WEU. While these forces have often been derided as political tokens that do not address operational needs, some of them have gained credibility, like Eurocorps, whose HQ was deployed to Kosovo and Afghanistan. As Giegerich and Wallace (2004) have argued, EU countries have proved in recent years capable of deploying the equivalent of its European Rapid Reaction Force of 60,000 troops.

EUROPEAN DEFENCE AS A SOCIAL FIELD

To sum up, ESDP may not be a single defence policy, but it is more than a bureaucracy. A fairly large number of actors are actively involved in ESDP policymaking, both in Brussels and in the capitals. While defence remains the preserve of member states, ESDP is aimed at following *European* foreign policy objectives. It is thus part of a larger debate about political integration, which constitutes for many its *telos*. That is why Jolyon Howorth (2000b) describes ESDP as a case of "supranational intergovernmentalism."

A field like ESDP generates policy outputs. These policies can take the form of legislation or, as in the case of ESDP, programs, informal regulations, the production of political symbols, and important decisions such as intervening abroad militarily. In particular, the European Defence Initiative launched in 1998 has led to a proliferation of committees, working groups, and panels where governmental and nongovernmental actors try and influence the policy process. The European Capability Action Plan (ECAP), for instance, brings together military officers, defence planners, procurement directors, Commission officials, and industrialists who meet frequently as part of the EDA's Integrated Development Teams.

Of course, ESDP is a formal organization, with a Brussels-based bureaucracy of several hundreds officials, some of whom answer to European institutions, others to their national government. These actors meet in the COPS or in the Military Committee; they work together in the Military Staff or in the EDA. While the creation of these bodies is remarkable given the absence of military uniforms in EU buildings before 2000, the decision-making process remains crippled by the unanimity rule. The existence of 26 veto points (Denmark benefits from an opt-out clause) has often been identified as one of the main limits of European military integration. It also explains a tendency on the part of officials from the three military powers—France, the UK, and Germany—to caucus among themselves and act as a sort of ESDP vanguard, or *directoire*, with a view to breaking political impasses (Gegout 2002).

Domestic actors are therefore crucial. In this book, I usually focus on France, the UK, and Germany because their officials are perceived by their peers as the most important actors in the development of ESDP. In each of these three countries, European defence policy is formulated within a policy triangle consisting of international security and defence staff officials within the defence ministries; political directorates, CFSP, and international security diplomats within foreign ministries; and foreign and EU policy advisors within the executive branch. I will have more to say about these actors in Chapters 2 and 3.

But ESDP is also a set of informal networks. These, I argue, are structured enough around distinct stakes that they can be called a "field" in Bourdieu's sense. As I wrote in the Introduction, a field is structured space of relations, centred on agreed-upon stakes, functioning according to known if implicit rules, wherein actors draw on their "capital" as a resource to maintain their position in the field. Actors recognize each other as being involved in the same game; their interaction is fairly routinized; and there is a shared understanding of what the field is about, what the rules are, and what the hierarchy of actors is. The field is characterized by mostly shared social representations and often contested power structures. In addition to government actors, the ESDP field is characterized by the fairly strong involvement of academics, research institutes, and think tanks (Dumoulin et al. 2003). The EU has its own shop, the Paris-based Institute for Security Studies, whose yearly July Conference attracts many influential figures in the field. But ESDP has also been a magnet for nongovernmental outfits that frequently hold conferences and workshops, publish policy papers, and try to position themselves as key interlocutors for the EU in the policy process. The most active ones are the Centre for European Reform, the Royal Institute of International Affairs, and the International Institute for Strategic Studies in Britain; the *Fondation pour la recherche stratégique*, the *Institut des relations internationales et stratégiques*, and the *Institut français des relations internationales* in France; the *Stiftung Wissenschaft und Politik* and the *Deutsche Gesellschaft für Auswärtige Politik* in Germany; and the European Policy Centre, the International Security Information Service, the New Defence Agenda, and the George Marshall Fund in Brussels. Clingendael in the Netherlands and NUPI in Norway are also productive outlets.

Fields are certainly not devoid of conflict. Acting on orders from their respective governments, French and British delegates are often at odds over whether European defence should privilege decision-making *autonomy* or the improvement of military *capabilities*. But they are usually in agreement against the Germans or the Belgians who want to give a greater role to the Commission in security affairs. Here, the issue is really about the *finalité politique* of European defence: official positions are often embedded in decades-old national social representations about the role of the state. Also, diplomats and defence actors do not see eye-to-eye on the usefulness of ESDP: while COPS diplomats are tempted to launch EU operations whenever and wherever they can as a way to show the Europe's credibility, defence staffs often fear that they do not have enough resources to pay for what they see as foreign ministries' over-eagerness to raise the 12-star flag. Diplomats look for opportunities to value their political capital while soldiers are more interested in material capabilities. The EU's support to the AU in Sudan and the 2006 intervention in the Congo were decried by some military interviewees and commentators as a futile exercise in self-promotion on the part of the Council diplomats, who sometimes presented this crisis management operation as a "test" to prove the value of ESDP. Some defence officials, especially German ones, but also Commission officials were more than reluctant.[4] Launching an operation

---

[4] This reluctance was confirmed by three senior military officers interviewed at the EU Military Staff (2005) the UK Permanent Representation (2002) and the German Defence Ministry (2002). See also Jean-Yves Haine, Bastian Giegerich. "In Congo, a Cosmetic EU Operation," *International Herald Tribune.* 12 June 2006.

remains the most dramatic stake experienced in the European security and defence field. Not surprisingly, it leads to an intensification of social interaction.

Actors are endowed with varying resources to promote their views. Put in Bourdieusian terms, actors seek to convert their specific capital into symbolic and political capital. For example, diplomats were generally in the driver's seat of ESDP at the beginning, when the project was foreign policy-led and required political impetus and institutional foundations. But British defence officials had more of a say in the elaboration of their government's policy than their French counterparts did; they could draw on a comparatively greater social and cultural capital, shaped by a shared professional background and prestige, to influence the executive. To understand Britain's position towards European defence, one must compare the rather egalitarian relations prevailing between the Ministry of Defence and the Foreign Office to the French case, where the foreign ministry dominates the relationship.

That said, the relative value of resources changes as the field changes. As the capability agenda gained prominence with ECAP and, later, defence officials and military officers in particular were able to convert their specific expertise about these issues into political influence in London, Paris, and Brussels. In parallel fashion, when they got the chance, representatives from Nordic states and the Commission, as well as NGOs, tried to reorient ESDP in a way that enhanced the value of their "civilian resources." Today, there are still important struggles taking place in the transgovernmental field about whether ESDP should be foreign policy- or capability-led, and whether it should focus on military or civilian assets.

Taking a close look at the ESDP field thus provides a clue to a much debated issue. While most scholars call for the creation of a common European "strategic culture," they generally agree that, due to the resilience of national approaches, this culture has not penetrated member states yet (Rynning 2003; Meyer 2006). Having studied national responses to ESDP in Germany, Austria, the UK, and France, Bastian Giegerich (2006: 202) concludes that even though "the spectrum is narrowing, progress towards a common strategic culture has, thus far, been extremely limited." Yet, among ESDP *actors*, there clearly is a common set of social representations. By and large, all agree that ESDP is desirable; that it will be based on a

Franco-British compact with Germany as an occasional honest broker; that European countries must increase defence expenditures and rationalize their military tools; that good relations with the US are key to making ESDP work; and that the EU must use every available opportunity to demonstrate its military credibility on the ground. I never encountered any argument to the contrary on the part of ESDP actors. In other words, despite the legacy of national security cultures, ESDP actors share what Bourdieu calls "principles of vision and division" that underpin a common understanding of what ESDP is *about*—even though they may not agree on what it should *do*.

CONCLUSION

In an interview I did with Hubert Védrine, the former French foreign minister told me in a derisive tone that "European defence—and that's its main virtue—provokes cheers at any political rally. The number of people who find it interesting is disproportionate relative to its actual importance."[5] While this may be a bit exaggerated, it is true that many people pin high hopes on ESDP that perhaps it can never fulfill. The reason is simple: many believe that ESDP is the first step towards creating a truly European military organization, eventually a European army, realizing the EU founders' vision of a state-like federation (Salmon and Shepherd 2003).

While ESDP may never reach that goal, it has clearly become a strongly institutionalized transgovernmental field, where hundreds of actors interact frequently, social practices are produced, and power structures are reproduced. The fact that actors clash over policy and symbolic issues demonstrates that, for them, European defence matters; it also suggests that cleavages are not only national (which would substantiate the intergovernmentalist thesis) but also often professional and ideological (which lends credence to the argument that ESDP has its "own" social representations). From a historical perspective, the existence of a transgovernmental arena wherein sovereign states coordinate and pool their military

---

[5] Interview, Paris, 2005.

capabilities in the name of a regional foreign policy stands out as an anomaly.

In the remainder of this book, I probe how such a field was created. To do so, I go back to the development since the early 1950s of an international defence and a European foreign policy field. The history of these two fields, I argue, explains both why ESDP was created and how this new field is structured.

2

The Internationalization of European Armed Forces

When one thinks of globalization, the military is probably not the first institution that comes to mind. As I argued in the Introduction, armed forces are intimately linked to the formation and consolidation of national states. It was France's King Charles VII who, in 1439, established the first permanent army. Professional armies spread throughout Europe in the seventeenth century, precisely when the Westphalian system of state sovereignty was being put in place. Originating in the *levée en masse* mobilized by revolutionary France against continental enemies, conscription and the mass army model had been adopted by virtually every European country by the end of the nineteenth century (Ralston 1966; Parker 1996). The national link between the citizen and the state was strengthened with the creation of military academies, war memorials, and state rituals honouring national victories.

Despite this strong national heritage, the European military was by the turn of the twenty-first century one of the most internationalized organizations. For King (2005: 333), "The armed forces of Europe are becoming transnational because this is the only way that states—and the armed forces themselves—can address security threats in the current era." Although I do not necessarily agree with the sense of inevitability implied, King's argument illustrates that the interpenetration of European armed forces is deeper than that of most multinational corporations. The practices of military actors are becoming quite uniform, their language common, and their missions are only rarely associated to national defence *stricto sensu*. This has even led some scholars to speak of a "cosmopolitan" or a "postmodern" military, of which European forces would display the most advanced form.

In this chapter, I argue that this sea change can be attributed to the creation, since the end of World War II, of an international defence field, with its own rules and structures, and centred primarily but not exclusively on Europe. The progressive institutionalization of military cooperation has gone hand in hand with the consolidation of an international defence field. I first explain how international military cooperation developed from 1945 to the 1990s. Taking place in NATO, military-to-military interaction expanded after 1989 with the increasing frequency of multinational operations abroad. While institutional or political integration was never stated as an explicit goal, NATO thus produced a kind of diffuse spillover that made further cooperation increasingly compelling (and isolation increasingly costly), with the result that, today, no European state is engaged in a nonmultinational operation overseas and most neutral countries are rethinking their relationship to NATO. Then, I provide evidence that a strongly institutionalized international defence field does indeed exist today. In particular, I look at the involvement and level of interaction of military actors in the field; the convergence of practices and social representations; and the reproduction of power structures within the field.

STRUCTURES OF MILITARY COOPERATION IN EUROPE

The Western Union

Until 1947, the main causes of concern for Britain and France, Europe's two victorious but battered powers, remained their respective colonial empires and Germany. In March 1947, after French Communists and General de Gaulle, who was wary of France's military dependence on Britain given their rivalry in the Levant, left the coalition government, Paris and London signed the Treaty of Dunkirk, a bilateral defence assistance pact specifically aimed at preventing Germany's resurgence. This treaty included some provisions for defence cooperation as well, but its ambitions remained modest and limited to the event of a German attack on French soil. Worried by colonial unrest, Britain did not want to commit to the defence of Europe. The British defence establishment in particular was skeptical towards Franco-British cooperation, which they saw as answering the Foreign Office's political considerations rather than fulfilling Britain's strategic interests. The opposite was true in France, where the armed forces were more enthusiastic about cooperating with the comparatively stronger British military (Decup 1998: 187ff).

The Communist-led overthrow of the democratic government in Czechoslovakia and the Berlin blockade in early 1948 triggered a reconsideration of the countries' security policies (Judt 2006: 129ff). Negotiations between France, Britain, and the Benelux led to the signing of the Treaty of Brussels in 1948. Within the Western Union that this treaty created a mutual guarantee of automatic assistance between the signatories was introduced to deal with the emerging Soviet threat: Article V, which is still in force in a modified Brussels treaty. Germany was excluded from the defence pact but, apart from small French circles, it was no longer seen as the most likely threat. The signatories agreed to share information, exchange military personnel and *matériel*, and coordinate their defence policies. Common planning and joint manoeuvres were envisaged. For the first time in conditions of peace, a small military staff and a Chiefs of Defence committee were established in Fontainebleau.

Unsure of each others' reliability, London and Paris quickly turned to Washington for additional support. In late 1947, British Foreign Secretary Ernest Bevin had suggested to George Marshall, the US Secretary of State, that a transatlantic alliance be set up (Dumoulin and Remacle 1998; Rees 1998). After an acrimonious "great debate" on Capitol Hill, the North Atlantic (Washington) Treaty was signed in April 1949 between Brussels Pact members, the US, and Canada. A Western bloc was firmly in place, as the US had abandoned its century-old skepticism towards "entangling" alliances. But military *integration* was not yet high on the agenda.

The EDC

The Korean War broke out in June 1950. US defence planners quickly came to the conclusion that, in order to make Western defence effective,

Germany had to rearm (Duffield 1995: 33). The Truman administration insisted that, in the absence of genuine European cooperation within the Alliance, the US would defend the Rhine, not the Elbe. By and large, the French military concurred, but several politicians remained adamantly opposed because they thought that the Alliance "did not offer adequate guarantees against a rearmed Germany" (Aybet 2001: 72). A circle of officials around Jean Monnet, a French civil servant, exploited this opportunity and proposed a European plan, based on the Coal and Steel Community model, that would address US strategic concerns and French fears of German rearmament. The plan championed by Prime Minister René Pleven and Foreign Minister Robert Schuman would come to be known as the EDC.

The idea was to incorporate Western European armed forces, including that of Germany and Italy, within multinational command structures in a French-dominated organization. These structures would be integrated at the level of relatively small combat teams, which precluded the formation of German-only divisions. There would be a commissariat, modeled after the ECSC's High Authority, to deal with strategic command and procurement; a Council of Defence Ministers with a European Minister of Defence; and, eventually, a common budget. Initially, the plan even proposed that 15% of each country's contribution to the common budget should be spent in other EDC countries. In spite of the logistical challenges it entailed, the EDC plan was backed by the US as a second-best solution to German rearmament. Arguing that "their own global obligations precluded involvement," the British would not participate in what Churchill called a "sludgy amalgam," but they backed the plan (Rees 2001: 51).

Signed in 1952, the Treaty of Paris creating the EDC was torpedoed by the French National Assembly in 1954 (Aron and Lerner 1956; Parsons 2004). "The French government," later wrote Jean Monnet (1976: 406), "thought that the realization of the Coal and Steel Plan would allow minds to get used to the idea of a European Community before we would get to the delicate issue of common defence. Events did not give us enough time." Left with no other option, the French government came to accept the accession of Germany and Italy to the Western Union, which became the WEU, and to the Atlantic Alliance.

NATO

In spite of its failure, the EDC had one lasting impact: that of giving legitimacy to the notion of integrating European armed forces. Indeed, as the EDC debate was raging in France, the US and the UK were busy setting up credible military structures to buttress the Washington Treaty. The organization chart of the first EDC plan and Western Union structures were used as blueprints for these bodies. In 1949, only the political North Atlantic Council and the Military Committee were in place. But a year later, under the pressure of the Korean War, Allies created an integrated chain of command that was to be activated in the event of a Soviet attack. The post of Supreme Allied Commander, Europe (SACEUR), was established and granted to General Eisenhower. It became the rule that SACEUR would always be an American officer double-hatted as Commander of US Forces in Europe, and his deputy a European officer. In 1951, a military staff with strategic planning and operational capacity, SHAPE, was inaugurated in Rocquencourt, near Paris. A Defence Planning Group was set up and the North Atlantic Council was reorganized: delegates from various government departments (foreign affairs, defence, finance, etc.) were replaced by Permanent Representatives with broad competences and chaired by a Secretary General.

No longer a paper alliance, the North Atlantic Treaty now truly had an "organization," the first large-scale permanent multinational one in peacetime (Weber 1992). Regional commands were put in place under SACEUR: for the Channel (CINCHAN), Northern Europe (CINCNORTH), Southern Europe (CINCSOUTH), Central Europe (CINCENT), and the High-Wycombe Air Command. Conventional forces were built up according to a coordinated force planning process. At a meeting held in Lisbon in 1952, NATO ministers "set NATO force goals of fifty allied divisions, 4,000 aircraft, and substantial additional targets for future years" (Sloan 2002: 24). While "the Allies never reached these so-called Lisbon goals," they quickly established an extended system of forces in Central Europe. As Table 2.1 shows, around 1 million military personnel (between 20 and 28 divisions) operating under NATO control were permanently stationed in the region between 1960 and 1990.

As part of a deal to get France to accept the accession of Germany to NATO, British Foreign Secretary Anthony Eden pledged that Britain would station four divisions and an airforce in Europe for a period of 50 years. He also convinced the US to commit firmly to the defence of Europe, thus giving the French the security guarantee they had asked for during EDC talks. Germany, in turn, was allowed to recreate its armed forces under SACEUR command if Bonn formally renounced to produce nuclear weapons (Duffield 1995: 104ff). For the next 40 years or so, NATO became the focus of West European defence policies, and the nexus of their armed forces' interaction. Common operating standards were designed, attempts were made to coordinate combat support functions, and some common assets were established, such as the fleet of Airborne Warning and Control System (AWACS) reconnaissance planes. Chiefs of Defence interacted frequently through the Military Committee. An increasing number of military officers from all NATO countries came to work in SHAPE and in the International Military Staff. The original membership was expanded to Norway, Portugal, Greece, Turkey, Spain, and, after 1999, most of Eastern Europe. The only exceptions were the neutral countries (Ireland, Austria, Sweden, Finland) and, after 1966, France.[1]

France was always an awkward partner in NATO (Menon 2000). Paris' misgivings about US domination in the Atlantic Alliance were aroused by the 1956 Suez crisis, when Washington refused to support the Franco-British intervention. Relations deteriorated after De Gaulle came back to office in 1958. He began by withdrawing a certain number of French units from the SACEUR integrated command: the Mediterranean Fleet in 1959, Algerian divisions in 1962, and the entire navy in 1963. Conflicts around nuclear doctrine arose after France got its independent nuclear deterrent (Heuser 1997). In 1966, France left the military bodies of NATO: SACEUR, the Military Committee, the Defence Planning Group, and the Nuclear Planning Group. It remained, however, a member of NATO's political bodies. Through the Ailleret–Lemnitzer and Valentin–Farber agreements, it was agreed that France's integration in the military command would be left to its own choosing in the event of a crisis. But NATO forces had to leave French territory. As a consequence, NATO moved its offices from France to Belgium. Allied headquarters were established in Brussels and SHAPE in Mons.

---

[1] Spain did not join the integrated military structure until 1995 either.

Table 2.1. NATO force levels in Europe (1960–90)

	United Kingdom	France	Germany	Belgium	Netherlands	US	Canada	Total
1960								
Divisions	$3^3/_3$	2	7	2	2	5	1/3	$21^4/_3$
Military personnel[i]	64	72	270	120	135	237	9	907
1970								
Divisions	3	2	12	2	2	$4^3/_3$	1/3	$25^4/_3$
Military personnel[i]	60	62	466	95	121	213	5	1,022
1980								
Divisions	4	3	12	2	2	$4^5/_3$	1/3	$27^6/_3$
Military personnel[i]	66	47	495	88	115	244	5	1,060
1990								
Divisions	3	3	12	2	2	$4^4/_3$	1/3	$26^5/_3$
Military personnel[i]	64	53	461	92	103	244	7	1,024

[i] In thousands. Figures do not include reserve or territorial force.

Source: Duffield (1995: 234).

Franco-German and Other Forms of Bilateral Cooperation

While most military-to-military cooperation took place within NATO and in a large number of NATO bases, Franco-German cooperation deserves a separate discussion. Withdrawal from NATO came as something of a shock for the French military. "From 1942 to 1966," writes a historian, "French armed forces were one of the most evident instruments of Americanization. In one generation, a process of deep acculturation developed" (Vial 2002: 6–7). To a large extent, this social capital was lost after 1966. French officers left NATO headquarters; although the airforce kept close relations with the Americans and the British, other services were rather isolated in terms of training or exercises, which from the 1960s to the 1980s were mostly conducted with colleagues from the former colonies. As the French were excluded from the international defence field, their doctrines became increasingly idiosyncratic (with a strong focus on nuclear deterrence) and equipment standards diverged. By the turn of the 1990s, it was a commonly lamented fact that French soldiers had not developed their English skills as much as other Europeans, which made cooperation on the ground difficult.

Military authorities, however, continued to promote informal forms of cooperation with the Allies. As William Wallace (1986: 236) writes:

the gap which therefore opened up between doctrine and practice, and between political rhetoric and the preferences and assumptions of the military, led to a certain *engrenage* between French military commanders and the NATO structure which, given its extreme political sensitivity in French domestic politics, became in the late 1970s one of the most carefully suppressed aspects of European defence cooperation. Informal contacts, observer status in Alliance discussions and joint training naturally brought the French closer to the Germans than to the British. French forces were in south-western Germany, British forces in northern; the non-official character of French cooperation with other forces naturally placed a greater emphasis on bilateral, rather than multilateral, collaboration.

Even before France withdrew from the integrated command, it had started to develop a strategic relationship with Germany through the 1963 Elysée Treaty of Friendship and Reconciliation. The treaty provided for a modicum of military-to-military cooperation. Several joint procurement projects, like the Transall aircraft and the Tiger combat helicopter, were developed under its umbrella. These provisions were given greater salience in the 1980s, when Paris and Bonn created a Franco-German Security and Defence Council and the Franco-German Brigade (Sauder 1995; Bloch-Laine 1999). The brigade, made up of 4,500 soldiers of whom 750 were assigned to mixed companies, was upgraded to a European Corps in 1992. Incorporating Spanish, Belgian, and Luxembourg troops in 1995, the Eurocorps was slowly brought into the remit of SACEUR. While this link with NATO was supposed to be operational only in the event of a military crisis, the frequency of multinational operations in the 1990s quickly meant that this would be more than just a theoretical possibility. "As the 1990s went on," concludes Charles Cogan (2001: 72), "the French were becoming acquainted with NATO operationally on the ground and in combat zones."

Uniquely embodied by the Franco-German Brigade in 1988, and to some extent by the Allied Command Europe Mobile Force, bi- and multi-national forces became ubiquitous in the following decade. As Thomas-Durrell Young (2001: 198) quips, their creation owed more to a "tremen-dous political cachet" than to any real operational value added. The idea of creating a host of multinational units was introduced at the 1990 NATO Summit in London, very much at Germany's insistence, which then "assumed the lion's share (at division or corps level) of all large European multinational forces" (Fleckenstein 2000: 81). Suffice it to mention the two US-German Corps, the German-Dutch Corps, the Northeast German-Danish-Polish Corps, and the Multinational Division (Central). Britain is the lead nation in the Allied Command European Rapid Reaction Corps. These forces complement NATO's common assets, such as the AWACS reconnaissance fleet (Baumann 2001).

FROM STRUCTURES TO ACTION

By 1989, there was in Europe what looked like a strongly institutionalized international defence field. The field was centred on NATO, where force planning was coordinated, procedures were standardized, and strategic and tactical decisions were made. On the ground, the impact of NATO was felt in its myriad Europe-based HQs and bases. While most bases were national as forces were stationed alongside one another in a "layer cake" pattern, combined exercises and manoeuvres were commonplace, and NATO headquarters were multinational. With the notable exception of France and neutral countries, every European or Canadian unit, as well as a good number of US troops, was governed by a planning process decided in Brussels for the defence of Western Europe. The irony is that this dense institutional structure was never put to use.

This started to change after the end of the Cold War, when the international community began to take on an increasing number of peace support operations. Multinational expeditionary missions were not new, and there had often been, at least rhetorically, an element of "peace restoration." The first one of this kind in the modern era was the Franco-British expedition in Crimea, in 1853–6. Since 1956, European and North American troops had been involved in a series of peacekeeping operations under the auspices of the UN. In Cyprus, Lebanon or Sinai, soldiers from France, the UK, or the Netherlands wore the same blue helmet.

But 1989 brought about a qualitative change. Bastian Giegerich and William Wallace (2004: 179) estimate that "European governments collectively have doubled the number of troops deployed abroad within the past decade." Between 1989 and 1995, for example, French military expenditures for foreign operations were multiplied by three (Paulmier 1997). In the late 1990s, 25–47% of British military personnel were deployed abroad (Freedman 2001: 303). The early 1990s are replete with low intensity (although not low casualty) conflicts in which European countries got involved under a UN flag: Cambodia, Somalia, Rwanda, Yugoslavia.

Soon, however, it appeared that greater military efficacy was required in places like Bosnia, and NATO was called in. Western countries lowered their contribution to UN operations, but increased significantly their assignment of troops to NATO operations, thus furthering the regionalization of the European military. The overwhelming majority of European troops abroad were committed to NATO operations around the turn of the century (Giegerich and Wallace 2004).

These foreign deployments, either in UN or in NATO context, had important consequences from the standpoint of multinational cooperation. In Bosnia's UN Protection Force, for example, French, British, and Dutch soldiers learned to work together. Their military traditions, forged by years of colonial experience, proved in fact quite similar. They shared a commitment to peace support operations but also muscular methods linked to expeditionary warfare, even though these may have been at odds with the UN's stringent rules of engagement. The French also realized that their deficient knowledge of English and NATO procedures posed real problems to their integration with foreign troops in multinational contexts. In a well-known example, Philippe Morillon, the French UNPROFOR Commander, insisted on using NATO procedures. The British, for their part, "shared irritation at the preoccupation of US forces with self-protection at the expense of other operational goals" (Giegerich and Wallace 2004: 166).

THE INTERNATIONAL DEFENCE FIELD

The story of European militaries in the second part of the twentieth century is one of ever deepening integration. As I wrote at the outset, this was an unintended consequence ("diffuse spillover," so to speak) of the need to defend Europe collectively against the Soviet Union. To what extent does it make sense to speak of an "international defence" field? While the boundaries of a field are always somewhat porous, the international defence field is better structured than most by having NATO as its institutional core. While the organization is transatlantic, it involves rather more Europeans than Americans today: most European soldiers are likely to have participated in a NATO operation but only a small minority of US soldiers are. Embodying a common set of social representations in many respects, the international defence field has also been, at times, a deeply fractious one.

NATO is the locus of an intense social interaction on transatlantic strategic issues; for nearly 50 years, it is where West European and North American governments have shaped their collective defence posture, discussed joint military undertakings, and settled divergences on strategic issues (Risse-Kappen 1995). It is also where defence planners have met to coordinate their national defence policies and agree on a common force planning process (Morgan 2003). Finally, NATO is the instrument they have used to prepare and conduct allied military exercises and, after 1990, multinational operations. In Western Europe and

Canada, there are few aspects of defence policy that have been left untouched by the interaction taking place in this international defence field.

In this section, we will take a look at who the actors of the international defence field are, what social representations they share and do not share, and which power structures help us explain the field's dynamics.

Actors

By international organization standards, NATO is a huge organization. Four thousand people work in its Brussels headquarters alone. Of these, 2,100 officials, civilian and military, work in the national delegations representing 26 member states. The remaining 2,000 are employed directly by the organization; they are often seconded from the member states on a fixed-term basis. But the international defence field extends far beyond NATO headquarters. According to its own estimates, NATO employs ~5,200 civilian staff worldwide. NATO also coordinates literally hundreds of policy committees, organizations, and agencies, where officials and military officers from the member states meet to discuss issues ranging from meteorology to logistics to nuclear forces to helicopter design to computer standardization. As we will see in the next chapter, only the EU can claim such extensive transgovernmental networks.

NATO is divided in two organizational lines. The *political* side is centred on the North Atlantic Council, where foreign ministers (occasionally defence ministers or heads of government) meet, and the Defence Planning Committee (DPC), where defence ministers meet, on average twice a year. The NAC is where important strategic issues, such as whether to send NATO troops somewhere or how to define potential threats, are taken. The DPC is where Allied governments coordinate their defence policies and determine their force contributions to the Alliance. Throughout the year, these two decision-making bodies are attended by Permanent Representatives, "NATO ambassadors," who meet at least once a week. The NAC and the DPC are chaired by a Secretary General, currently Jaap de Hoop Scheffer. They are supported by an International Staff of 1,200 civilian officials.

The *military* side is centred on the Military Committee, which is responsible for NATO's military policy *stricto sensu*. Like the NAC or the DPC, the Military Committee is where Chiefs of Defence are supposed to meet regularly. But in practice, they delegate Military Representatives who are permanently based in Brussels. Supported by an International Military Staff of ~500 military officers, the Military Committee gives military advice to the NAC and the DPC; it oversees the defence planning process and, in the event of an operation, prepares operational plans and concepts of operations. Crucially, Military Representatives also act as a transmission belt between political decision-makers and a key duo of military actors: the two Strategic Commanders.

Strategic Commanders are responsible for planning and conducting NATO's exercises and operations. Currently, there are two: SACEUR, based in Mons, Belgium, and the Supreme Allied Commander Transformation (SACT), based in Norfolk, Virginia. SACEUR, an American General, conducts most Allied operations, such as in Kosovo or in Afghanistan. If the Americans are not involved, as in Bosnia since 2004, strategic command is vested upon his European deputy, DSACEUR.

To do his work, SACEUR has access to the world's most important multinational military planning staff: SHAPE. SHAPE, where 2,000 military officers work, is the tip of a chain of subordinate commands and joint headquarters, which are mostly located in Europe. The role of this headquarters is to coordinate national forces assigned to NATO and organize multinational exercises and operations. In this "integrated military structure," a British general can give orders to a German colonel, who will in turn have a Dutch lieutenant as his *aide de camp*. This implies that, every year, thousands of staff officers from NATO countries come in contact with each other and take instructions from each other. "Seconded civilian officials and military personnel from other NATO members," writes Anthony Forster, "work in planning staffs and defence policy departments and in each other's military HQ, which are increasingly multinational in terms of personnel" (Forster 2005: 148). In terms of military integration, there is no equivalent in the modern world. Few multinational corporations even have this level of social integration, involving daily interaction among thousands of defence actors.

While the command and control mechanism supervising joint operations or exercises is multinational, military forces remain for the most part national. For a career officer, national chains of command are always more compelling than multinational ones. Each country determines and maintains its contribution to NATO's force structure, which either stays home or is stationed abroad but on a separate base. Since the 1990s, however, there have been a growing number of multinational forces, where nationalities are integrated at the headquarters level, the list of which can be found in Table 2.2. Here again, the Germans have probably gone further than most: in addition to being involved in a number of multinational forces, like Eurocorps, Germany has gone out of its way to multinationalize its new operations headquarters. Based in Potsdam, the *Einsatzführungskommando* accommodates liaison officers from nine other countries and can be further augmented during operations.[2]

The rather rigid separation between political and military hierarchies in the Allied organization is replicated in the member state capitals. NATO policy is formulated by two distinct groups of actors, namely diplomats and defence officials responsible for political affairs, and defence staffs responsible for operational issues. Normally, the executive branch will host a secretariat to coordinate national positions and prepare Cabinet meetings: for example, the *Secrétariat général de la défense nationale* in France or the Defence and Overseas Secretariat in Britain.

Each foreign ministry normally has an international security branch. It is for example called Strategic Affairs and Security Directorate in the French *Quai d'Orsay* and International Security in the UK Foreign Office. These diplomats, who report to their ministry's political director, develop national positions on the Alliance's political issues, such as responses towards specific crises, accession of new members, or an assessment of NATO's mandate. In addition to appointing their country's Permanent Representative in the North Atlantic Council, foreign ministries are represented in Brussels through the Political Committee, the senior foreign policy group which prepares NAC meetings. Kovanda estimates that between 25,000 and 30,000 documents circulate among the national delegations and NATO every year (cited in Forster 2005: 148).

Defence ministries also have civilian officials in charge of NATO policy. In France, the Strategic Affairs Delegation reports directly to the minister; in Britain, there is a NATO/European Policy Group in the Security

---

[2] Interview, Bundesministerium der Verteidigung, Berlin, 2002.

Table 2.2. List of multinational forces in Europe

Type	Name	Headquarters
Lead nation/framework nation	ACE Rapid Reaction Corps	Mönchengladbach, Germany
	First United Kingdom Armoured Division	Herford, Germany
	Third United Kingdom Division	Bulford, UK
	Third Italian Division	Milan, Italy
Binational Formations	I German/Netherlands Corps	Münster, Germany
	V US/German Corps	Heidelberg, Germany
	II German/US Corps	Ulm, Germany
Multinational formations	Allied Land Forces Schleswig-Holstein and Jutland (LANDJUT)/Multinational Corps Northeast	Rendsburg, Germany
	Multinational Division (Central)	Mönchengladbach, Germany
	European Corps	Strasbourg, France
	European Rapid Operational Force (EUROFOR)	Florence, Italy

Source: Young (2001: 217).

Department. Through the Defence Review Committee, the defence equivalent of the Political Committee, these civilian officials are mostly involved in the defence planning process; that is, coordinating national defence policies and determining NATO's force posture. These officials will also brief their defence minister for occasional DPC and NAC meetings.

The final group of actors consists of military officers themselves. Defence staffs are heavily involved in the operational dimension of NATO policy, notably the force planning process (i.e. determining which forces will be assigned to NATO) and operational issues (i.e. which forces will be deployed on a NATO operation). Some defence staffs, like France's Euro-Atlantic Division may also play a more political role in shaping their country's NATO policy.

Social Representations

For Bourdieu, actors embody social dispositions that are structured by their place and trajectory in a social field. *Habitus*, as he calls them, are prereflexive, practice-oriented *social representations* that come from socialization and are physically embodied in the actor's attitude, or *hexis*. For 400-odd years, European military actors were immersed in national fields of power. Whether couched in defensive or expansionary terms, the purpose of armed forces was national security. Organizational formats varied widely, between the mass land army format of France and the more flexible, navy-based posture of the UK. Around the turn of the twentieth century, the continental defensive military doctrine of, say, France, was very different from the offensive one of its neighbour, Germany (Posen 1984; Kier 1997). However, France and Britain had large colonial empires to maintain while the military reach of most European countries was limited to the continent. In sum, the social representations of military actors were bounded by a national security culture (Katzenstein 1996).

To the extent that an international defence field has been institutionalized, we should observe a convergence of these social representations towards a transnational NATO culture stressing collective (as opposed to strictly national) security, multinational cooperation, and a common model of professional forces fit for overseas crisis management. This convergence has been well established so far as NATO delegates in Brussels are concerned (Gheciu 2005). I would argue that while there is still a great deal of diversity among European armed forces, there has also been a convergence of military representations around the "culturally interoperable professional" *habitus* promoted by NATO.

It is indeed striking how similar in outlook European armed forces have become since the early 1990s. In particular, Moskos, Allen, and Segal (2000) identify the pre-eminence in Western military practice of "operations other than war, authorized by entities beyond the nation state," and leading to the "internationalization of military forces themselves." Elliot and Cheeseman (2004) even go further and discern the emergence of a "cosmopolitan-minded," if not "cosmopolitan" yet, military. These characteristics have been associated to a shift from pre-1989 territorial defence to post-1990 force projection. The prerequisite for these changes has been the development of a professional soldier model, based less on a low-skilled mass army driven by patriotism and more on a high-skilled, flexible force available for changing goals, often multinational in character.

To be sure, European armed forces remain very diverse in their strength, composition, and ethos. The British and French stand apart with their focus on expeditionary warfare and their desire to maintain the full spectrum of violence, including nuclear weapons. By contrast, smaller European countries, but also bigger ones like Italy and Germany, have come, with unequal means, to brace themselves for international but low-intensity operations, like peacekeeping. In particular, these "late modern" forces, as Forster calls them, have given up or reduced their reliance on conscription. Neutral countries, however, like Ireland and Austria, have retained it. They remain very much focused on traditional territorial defence, often through militia systems, and thus with weak projection capabilities.

NATO's unified command and planning capabilities have, in the words of Terry Terriff (2004: 120), facilitated "the development of a common security and defence culture. This commonality contributed to the denationalization of security and defence planning, as member states increasingly developed their security and defence planning in relation to NATO's common defence planning process." Of course, this common NATO culture is generated by the drafting and adoption of common documents, notably the Strategic Concept, "the authoritative statement of the Alliance's objectives [which] provides the highest level of military guidance on the political and military means to be used in achieving them." But as important are the numerous *loci* of daily interaction where shared visions are produced and common practices reproduced. As a German airman who had served on a string of NATO posts confided to me, "We [pilots] understand each other." By that, he acknowledged that professional dispositions transcended national allegiance.

To determine which "political and military means" can and will be used, NATO relies on a very extensive defence and force planning process. While member states are free to decide their contribution to the Alliance, they have to coordinate their national defence plans with Allies and, in cooperation with NATO's Strategic Commands, agree on force planning goals for the Alliance. This cooperation involves logistics, standardization, nuclear planning, rules of engagement, crisis management procedures, and so on (Tuschhoff 1999: 146). The defence planning cycle involves a constant sharing of information in places such as SHAPE, multinational force headquarters, the Military Committee, the Defence Review Committee, or the Committee of National Armaments Directors.

In addition, the international defence field is crisscrossed by numerous institutions specifically designed to foster a NATO culture, such as the NATO Defence College in Rome or exchange programmes for military officers. For Donna Winslow and Peer Everts (2001: 87–8), these institutions have served to promote a "NATO military culture," which:

centres on the notion of a "military profession": the organised body of persons holding expertise in a set of closely related techniques or practices for "managing"—i.e. handling, transforming, constructing—violence. Despite the fact that military personnel represent separate states (and belong to different national-military traditions), NATO has a very large array of arrangements for exchanging information about military techniques, assuring that the interests and status of NATO are guaranteed; creating and recreating a NATO identity and establishing criteria for admission, training and co-ordination within the organization.

The multinational operations of the last decade have reinforced the trend in Europe towards increased multinational cooperation on the basis of a common professional ethos. With the exception of French and British interventions in Africa, overseas military operations in the 1990s were exclusively led by relatively small forces operating in coalition frameworks. As Thomas (2000: 10) writes, "this demands more integrated communications, command and control systems. Whereas during the Cold War, Allied forces would have been integrated at the corps or air-force-wing level, today's coalitions often come together at brigade or air-squadron level, placing a high premium on interoperability."

Interoperability is the technical ability to coordinate different weapons and communications systems. Sloan notes that it has become key to military practices: "The NATO focus on interoperability and on the development of habits of cooperation in both political and military relations makes operations among the forces of NATO members possible" (Sloan 2002: 192). Military sociologists who have studied multinational operations have observed that success is partly predicated on the quality of *human* cooperation among soldiers from different countries. They call this requirement *cultural* interoperability.

Cultural interoperability is a key *modus operandi* of the international defence field, to which it gives much of its symbolic texture. It takes many forms, such as the development of common communications systems and the convergence of rules of engagement. To give one example, an area where NATO has had the most profound impact is in the widespread adoption of the English language. Ten years ago, the French defence ministry realized that the lack of English skills among its officers and NCOs posed a huge problem because of the creation of multinational forces and the increasing number of international operations.[3] The Bosnian movie, *No Man's Land*, captured the tragic and hilarious implications of this problem: in a crucial scene, it shows well-intentioned French UN peacekeepers trying to solve a delicate situation between a Bosnian and a Serbian soldier who are stuck together in a trench; but they fail in large part because they are unable to communicate the complexity of the problem to their superiors in English.

---

[3] Interview, École supérieure militaire, Saint-Cyr-Coëtquidan, 2001.

Multilingual forces have existed throughout history. In the Roman Empire, although the official language of the legions was Latin, Greek was tolerated. The Habsburg and Ottoman empires had multilingual armies, while the navies of both were Italian-speaking. Today, Canada and Belgium have bilingual armed forces (Peled 2000). In some European units, such as the Franco-German Brigade or Eurocorps, there are several idioms. But in practice, in the Eurocorps HQ as in KFOR, English is the common working language. As a result, observes Forster, "proficiency in English as the language of international security missions is emerging as a prerequisite for commanders at all level" (Forster 2005: 71).

Cultural interoperability and professionalism are useful ways to address the question of whether there is a common strategic culture in the international defence field. The concept of strategic culture was introduced by Jack Snyder (1989) and Alastair Johnston (1995) to describe the ideals, responses, and patterns of habitual behaviour that members of a strategic community, or a field, share with each other. Cornish and Edwards (2001) used it to study NATO's and the EU's strategic cultures. Elizabeth Kier (1997), for her part, prefers the concept of "political–military culture" to explain French and British military doctrines between the two world wars. I concur with her that this is a more appropriate term for soldiers who are not in the business of deciding where and when they should come out of their barracks.

Most of the research on strategic or political–military culture has stressed how cultures differ from country to country, and thus help explain state behaviour. Cultural interoperability is about not harmonizing these cultures, but making them at least compatible. It supplements a common understanding of how armed forces should be organized to undertake crisis management operations: namely by transforming mass armies devoted to territorial defence into smaller, flexible packages of highly skilled, professional forces. While governments may have different readings of an international crisis and its role in the security environment, it is important that, on the ground, soldiers share a common professional ethos and work out ways to cooperate with each other, including by sharing a common vocabulary. For example, the few studies we have tend to show that military officers who believe in the importance of learning foreign languages and support the idea of "new international missions" are much more supportive of European defence (Mérand 2003; Bagayoko 2005*b*).

But language is not all there is. It is not surprising that, in almost every interview I conducted with French officers, they would talk of the British as peers. The British reaction was somewhat less sanguine but, often, both French and British derided the Germans, who they saw as a second-class army. While NATO experience should have brought the Germans and the British closer, the fact that the French and the British belonged to professional forces that are not combat-averse and that have a long history of counter-insurgency warfare was hailed as something that somehow made them—and only *them*, in Europe—comrades in arms.

In sum, while European armed forces remain diverse, social representations in the international defence field are converging around the template of the culturally interoperable professional soldier, who is skilled, flexible to work with fellow professionals from different countries, and is task-based rather than driven by patriotism. There may not be a common strategic culture but the political–military one is blooming. This convergence is largely the result of the development of a NATO culture and the multiplication of multinational operations, both of which are constitutive of the international defence field. "Where internationalization has had most reach," writes Forster (2005: 268), "is through NATO transmitting norms of professionalism, developing a common corpus of military doctrine, promoting interoperability and over quite a considerable period of time minimizing the fear of shared multinational command structures." This does not mean that European soldiers have become mercenaries, but rather that they have come to share a certain number of practices that are now part of their professional identity.

Power Structures

One could fill a library with books and pamphlets heralding the end of NATO. Since its inception, the Atlantic Alliance has been the subject of much speculation on its coming demise. This has to do with the fact that the international defence field is characterized by strong power asymmetries, which translate into political struggles over the purpose of the Atlantic Alliance, the strategies that it should adopt, and the way it should be organized in terms of hierarchy and membership.

In particular, two conflicts have structured NATO since its very beginning. The first is about the strategic goals of the Alliance. It often led to an exchange of bitter words about the *raison d'être* of the Alliance itself. In the pre-1989 era, when everybody agreed that the Soviet Union was the enemy, this conflict revolved around which defence doctrine served the Alliance best. It often pitted the US against the Europeans, who felt that Washington was forcing strategic concepts on its Allies that put their continent at risk. For example, says John Duffield, NATO adopted in the 1960s a nuclear strategy which sought to respond to an eventual Soviet nonnuclear aggression with conventional means, keeping nuclear retaliation as an option of last resort. "Flexible response" was a change from the previous strategy of massive retaliation in case of a Soviet strike. The Europeans feared that, because it lacked an adequate commitment on the part of the US to intervene with full force, this new strategy would encourage the Soviet Union to attack on the continent. "For the Europeans," remarks Duffield (1995: 242), "and especially the West Germans, who were on the front line, any war would assume near total proportions." The French were also suspicious of the US's nuclear strategy, an argument they used to justify their independent nuclear deterrent. The same sorts of debates reappeared in Western disputes around 1980, when the Soviet Union decided to deploy SS20 tactical weapons, which could reach Western Europe but not North America.

In the 1990s, as the nuclear issue became a less central one in the European security environment, the conflict over strategy moved to a different terrain, around the question of whether the Atlantic Alliance should stick to collective defence, the Article 5 option favoured by the French, or rather expand its reach to a variety of non-Article 5 crisis management missions, as Washington wanted. This conflict reached its apex under the George W. Bush administration, as French and Americans sparred over a possible NATO role in Iraq and the Sudan. Paris, discreetly supported by several European countries, argued that these non-Article 5 missions were not for NATO. They feared that European Allies would be instrumentalized as back up troops for US-led missions.

The second major conflict is about who should rule the international defence field. Here, we can observe three important cleavages. One cleavage has often pitted the most important military player, the US, against many Europeans. Since the 1950s, the French have been at the forefront of calls to rebalance decision-making in the Atlantic Alliance along two pillars, one North American and the other European. In recent years, this cleavage found a powerful expression in the enlargement debate, with Washington supporting a succession of enlargement rounds to East European, pro-American countries that some West European countries feared would dilute their influence in NATO (Schimmelfenning 2004).

Perhaps as important are the tensions between governments who believe they gain from the current distribution of responsibilities and governments who think they do not. For example, the US, the UK, and Germany are traditionally granted the top military positions in the SACEUR system, while countries like Spain or the Netherlands get political positions, like Secretary General or Chairman of the Military Committee, which are seen as somewhat less important. France, for its part, is excluded from the military hierarchy, and has rarely been given an important political position.

The third cleavage stems from the dual, political–military nature of the international defence field. This cleavage between diplomats and defence actors has often expressed itself in the form of a conflict between SACEUR, the US general who controls the integrated military structure, and the civilian hierarchy, either that of the Secretary General or that of the member states delegations. For all practical purposes, SACEUR is the most important official in the NATO hierarchy, being involved in every aspect of the Alliance's planning machinery and able to expect the support of national defence staffs, for whom the maintenance of NATO forces has become a "primary organizational mission" (Duffield 1995: 256). With the peace missions of the 1990s, however, diplomats have allegedly tried to increase their influence over SACEUR by micro-managing military operations through the NAC and the creation of new oversight and planning bodies (Vennesson 2000; Young 2001: 202).

These three cleavages sometimes overlap. For example, French officials, who are active in the political bodies but had for a long time excluded themselves from the military structure, have tended to view the SACEUR system with skepticism if not outright hostility. In the 1990s, France supported the idea of Europeanizing the military command as a way to rebalance the Alliance. Conversely, the Pentagon has often decried what it sees as the crippling influence of European diplomats, especially French diplomats, in the conduct of NATO operations.[4]

John Duffield argues that these intra-alliance differences are caused by two factors: one is geopolitical but the other is linked to military power asymmetries that are constitutive of the international defence field. In particular, he points out that influence is very much determined by how much capabilities and assets one contributes to the Atlantic Alliance. In principle, NATO's political decision-making structure operates on the basis of unanimity. Yet, the uneven distribution of military capabilities grants more bargaining power to some members at the expense of others. In that regard, the US military is quite simply in a league of its own. Its defence budget is twice that of all other NATO members combined. As Bosnia and Kosovo demonstrated, the US alone possesses some of the capabilities that NATO needs for large-scale operations, such as air power and precision-guided missiles. Countries like the UK, France, and Germany claim to compensate their relative technical weakness by contributing significantly more troops to NATO forces and operations. As a result, the transatlantic debate has often been framed in terms of "how the burden should be shared," namely whether equipment or troops matter more for the Alliance, and thus should yield influence.

As for other member states, they simply cannot hope to have a strong influence in the international defence field. One strategy followed by smaller countries has been to invest largely in the new multinational formations, which are good outlets for their "residual military capabilities" as well as opportunities to appoint officers to relatively senior command posts (Young 2001: 198). They can also join coalitions, like Belgium and Luxembourg frequently did with France, or exert some veto power, like Turkey and Greece are often tempted to do, but their position, and consequently that of their officials in the organization, is usually marginal even when their contribution in terms of personnel is not.

---

[4] See, for example, former SACEUR General Wesley Clark's recollections of his Kosovo experience in *Waging Modern War* (2001).

CONCLUSION

By the end of the twentieth century, the multinational military had become a reality in Western Europe. Armed forces exercised with each other regularly and operated abroad using shared assets with increasing frequency. Thousands of staff officers interacted in a number of multilateral organizations, primarily NATO. While military organizations remained shaped by national histories and the social representations of the national state, they were also converging towards a model of the culturally interoperable professional soldier. The "postmodern military," as Moskos, Allen, and Segal (2000) call it, "loosens the ties with the nation state, becomes multipurpose in mission, and moves towards a smaller volunteer force."

What took place in the international defence field had become an important element in the lives of ordinary soldiers. The vast majority of the missions they were deployed for (Bosnia, Kosovo, and later Afghanistan) were decided by the North Atlantic Council. The planning of national forces was coordinated by NATO's military bodies. The equipment and the procedures they used were in large part standardized through NATO's myriad institutions. Strong institutional links and cooperation habits were reinforced each time a new multinational operation was launched. Thanks to its planning and command structure, NATO became the most credible multinational military organization there ever was.

While transatlantic by birth, the international defence field involved European armed forces to a much greater extent than American ones. The US's immense military superiority and global reach drew a wedge between its armed forces and that of the Europeans. This capability gap meant that, even if the US remained a key player in NATO, the international defence field was increasingly a European one. A military officer quoted by Niagalé Bagayoko (2005*b*: 115) puts it eloquently: "Armed forces live Europe when they experience it on the field. The concrete experience of learning about new cultures and new ways of doing creates a common, European sense of belonging."

The development of a NATO military culture and strong interest on the part of European defence actors to keep NATO in place were, however, endangered by salient political conflicts over strategy, decision-making structures, membership, and purpose. Effective militarily, at least insofar as its members were, the international defence field faced an ever more daunting challenge of political legitimacy after the end of the Cold War. Before we turn to these events, let us take a look at what was happening on the diplomatic front during those years.

3

The Europeanization of Foreign Policy

One of the most prominent proposals in the failed *Treaty Establishing a Constitution for Europe* was the creation of a common diplomatic representation, the European External Action Service. The impetus behind the External Action Service was that the EU's foreign policy currently suffers from lack of both resources and coherence. Today, the conduct of the EU's external relations is split between the Commission, which conducts trade policy and provides development aid, and the Council, which controls more "political" aspects, including security and defence, but with a much smaller budget. In addition, the EU's foreign policy remains dependent on intricate forms of cooperation between EU institutions and national foreign ministries, which actually manage much wider networks of foreign delegations than Brussels. Member states do not have to agree on joint actions, and they can always defect from the common positions adopted in the Council of Ministers.

The Constitutional Treaty proposed to at least streamline the Brussels end of this complex architecture with the creation of a single EU foreign minister, who would have replaced the Commission's External Relations Commissioner and the Council's High Representative for the CFSP. The foreign minister would have chaired a Foreign Affairs Council. He or she would have relied on an integrated and expanded staff to support his or her action. The External Action Service would have been made up of officials from the Commission and the Council Secretariat, who currently work in separate offices and delegations abroad, as well as diplomats seconded from the member states. Needless to say, this EU diplomatic corps, a multinational body of hundreds of officials at the service of a regional organization, would have amounted to a revolution of sorts in the world of foreign policy.

While some argue that the EU foreign minister would have remained toothless vis-à-vis member states, especially France and Great Britain, two nuclear powers that hold permanent seats on the UN Security Council, others believe that the time is ripe for Europe to speak with one voice. The future probably lies in-between, as the creation of a beefed-up office of High Representative (but not a foreign minister) in the 2007 reform treaty suggests. In this chapter, I show that the past 50 years have resulted in the creation of what I call a *European foreign policy field*. To do so, I describe how the practices of European diplomats have been centred on, primarily, shaping the EU's internal affairs and, increasingly, enacting the EU's external relations. In other words, there has been twofold Europeanization. As Brian Hocking (2002) argues, European diplomats have come to act simultaneously as "gatekeepers" of the national interest in the EU and "boundary-spanners" of the European cooperative framework.

In the second part of the chapter, I argue that European diplomatic services have been integrated to a point where they now interact continuously and on a wide range of issues, sharing social representations and vying for influence over both the EU's foreign policy and the EU itself. These, I will argue, are characteristics of a highly structured, highly institutionalized social field. These diplomats have created a stock of institutional links and a culture of cooperation quite unparalleled in the rest of the world.

In a way, European diplomacy has always been about Europe. The continent is where diplomacy was born, first between Italian city states and then between the major European powers. The Concert of Europe, which emerged from the Congress of Vienna in 1815, formalized the practice of diplomacy which, until the late nineteenth century, remained largely confined to Europe, albeit also to some extent the US and Japan. Diplomacy then consisted in the posting of ambassadors and their staff in foreign capitals, where they would deliver *démarches*, interact with local authorities, and promote national interests in a strictly bilateral fashion (Neumann 2005; Cross 2006). As we will see, diplomacy in the EU now functions very differently.

SHAPING THE EU: THE INTERNAL DIMENSION

The post-World War II period was characterized by a multiplication of international and European organizations: the UN, NATO, the Organization for European Economic Cooperation, the Council of

Europe, to name only a few. But one organization more than any other, the EU, will become the centre of attention of European diplomats. Over the following 50 years, their main professional task will become one of "shaping the EU," of making sure that the institutional development of European cooperation and the policies undertaken by Brussels are favourable to the government they work for.

The forerunner of the EU, which adopted its current name only in 1993, was the European Coal and Steel Community. Established in 1951 by France, Germany, Italy, Belgium, the Netherlands, and Luxembourg, the ECSC permitted a joint regulation of the two industries most closely associated with war-making. To that effect, two institutions were created to exercise supranational authority over these key economic sectors: the High Authority, an "executive" body of nine independent *fonctionnaires* initially chaired by Jean Monnet, and the Court of Justice. A Special Council of (Economics) Ministers and a working-level Commission for the Coordination of the Council of Ministers (COCOR) were also created to ensure coordination with the member states. The US and the UK were the first nonmembers to establish missions (i.e. embassies) to the ECSC's headquarters in Luxembourg in 1952.

With the signing of the Treaty of Rome in 1957, the ECSC morphed into one of the three European Communities, with the new European Atomic Energy Community (EURATOM) and European Economic Community (EEC). The Common Market, a wide-reaching project of economic and political integration, was born. Its new institutions were to be based in Brussels rather than Luxembourg where, however, the High Authority and the Court of Justice stayed. Its progressive institutionalization in the 1960s was driven by a creeping assertiveness on the part of the institutions created by the ECSC and modified by the Treaty of Rome. In separate rulings, the European Court of Justice affirmed its authority to bypass national governments in order to reach out directly to private parties (*direct effect*) as well as the primacy of EU law over national law (Mattli and Slaughter 1998; Weiler 1999). The Council of Ministers worked towards an expansion of the practice of QMV on issues of Community competence— a practice that was temporarily halted by the "empty chair crisis" provoked by de Gaulle in 1965. In 1967, the ECSC High Authority and the Euratom Commission were merged with the EEC Commission, thus giving the EU a single executive. The European Parliament, based in Strasbourg, was transformed into an elected body in 1979, and saw its legislative power expand increasingly thereafter.

From the point of view of foreign ministries, an important development was the appointment, in 1958, of Permanent Representatives in Brussels. Together, they form COREPER, the Committee of Permanent Representatives, which replaced the ECSC's COCOR. These ambassadors to the EU prepare the agenda of Council meetings. They are both the voice of member states in Brussels and their member states' most senior EU experts. As such, they are located at the core of the EU's decision-making process (Lewis 2003; Menon 2004). While the Special Council of Ministers of the ECSC was made up of economics ministers, the post-Rome Council consists of different "formations" (transport, finance, etc.) of which the General Affairs formation, where foreign ministers meet, is the dominant one. Through the Permanent Representations in Brussels, diplomats have played a key if not *the* central role in shaping EU policy.

By the early 1970s, the basic institutional architecture of the EU was in place. The so-called institutional "triangle" consists of a supranational executive with the exclusive right of initiative in areas of Community competence, the Commission; an intergovernmental Council of Ministers to ensure member state approval of the Commission's initiatives; and a European Court of Justice to adjudicate in conflicts of competence between European institutions, between European and national levels of government, and between private parties and either European institutions or member states. This institutional triangle absorbed successive waves of enlargement: to the UK, Ireland, and Denmark in 1973; to Greece in 1981; to Spain and Portugal in 1986; to Sweden, Austria, and Finland in 1995; to eight former Communist countries plus Malta and Cyprus in 2004; and to Bulgaria and Romania in 2007.

In spite of their economic vocation, all of these institutions were created by diplomats. One reason was that, because European institutions entailed legal commitments and even some delegation of sovereignty on the part of the contracting parties, they required the signing of international treaties. The other reason was that they were seen as ultimately serving political objectives (Parsons 2004; Jabko 2006).

The ECSC and the Common Market were created by treaty. This became the standard way of altering, and more often than not expanding the scope of, European institutions. The 1987 Single European Act led to the completion of the single market and its "spillover" into new EU areas of competence, such as consumer policy, the environment, or labour standards. The 1993 Maastricht Treaty was associated with the insertion of two new "pillars": Justice and Home Affairs and the CFSP. The treaty also gave the regional organization its current name, the EU. More importantly, it launched the single currency, what is now the Euro. The 1997 Amsterdam Treaty led to new incursions in judicial and police cooperation and to the creation of a High Representative in charge of foreign policy. The 2001 Nice Treaty led to the establishment of the European security and defence policy. Each treaty usually led to an expansion of the powers of the European Parliament as well as a redistribution of votes and an extension of QMV within the Council of Ministers.

As Andrew Moravcsik (1998) has argued, these treaties can be understood as the "major turning points" of European integration. They are prepared by convening intergovernmental conferences. IGCs, as they are known, are negotiating forums that can last several months and bring together hundreds of diplomats and jurists from the capitals with a mandate from their governments to draft amendments to EU treaties. Negotiations are normally carried out by Permanent Representatives, who act as the personal envoys of their foreign ministers. An IGC culminates in a summit where the draft treaty is signed by heads of state or government. The first IGC was held in 1957 and led to the founding of the Common Market. Between 1958 and 1985 there was no IGC, but six such conferences were held between 1985 and 2004. The last one, in 2007, dealt with the reform treaty drafted to salvage the core elements of the Constitutional Treaty that failed to be ratified after negative French and Dutch referendums.

Even when there is no treaty in the making, much of Europe's diplomatic activity takes place around the preparation of European Council summits. The European Council, which is composed of all heads of state or government in addition to the president of the Commission, provides political direction to the EU. Formally, it meets twice a year, at the end of each six-month presidency of the EU but, in fact, it is more likely to meet four times a year. European summitry has allowed foreign ministries to remain in the driving seat of the EU's institutional development despite having been sidelined from most technical aspects of EU decision-making, especially in the economic area.

IGCs and summits are not the only events when European diplomats interact. Much of the interaction takes place daily in Brussels. The stake here is to shape EU policy in general: so-called "low politics" as opposed to the high politics of treaty change. Whether it is the environment or transport, policy initiatives are usually prepared by working groups made up of experts from specialized ministries and the Commission. But before they are seen by the relevant formation of the Council of Ministers, such initiatives must be vetted by COREPER. These "ambassadors to the EU" are normally career diplomats. They are also the heads of their country's biggest foreign delegation: the Permanent Representation.

Permanent Representations are the permanent bureaucratic link between Brussels and the member states' capitals. They house all national government officials posted in Brussels. Through working groups and committees, national experts participate in the formulation of EU policy; they negotiate on behalf of their government; and they keep their government informed of the Commission's doings. Permanent Representations are huge. Mai'a Cross (2006: 141) notes that "Today, many member states have their largest representations in Brussels." And they keep growing in size and influence. As Table 3.1 further illustrates, Germany's *ständige Vertretung* has doubled between 1988 and 2000; meanwhile, the size of France's *Représentation* tripled. This, so far as one can tell, is not a matter of bureaucratic creep but the symptom of a real increase in the workload.

In sum, the foreign policy of European countries is increasingly about EU policy. The vast majority of diplomats will at some point in their career be involved in either charting the institutional development of the EU through summitry or in the daily, more mundane business of shaping EU policies to their government's advantage. Not a single domestic policy is insulated from EU regulations, directives, benchmarking, or coordination efforts. What differs from the past experience of European foreign ministries is that these intergovernmental relations take place in one location, Brussels, on a permanent basis and across a wide spectrum of policy issues, from fisheries to nuclear nonproliferation. Before the EU, a typical diplomat would be posted in a foreign capital, where he or she would make the occasional *démarche* on some political issue. The EU has revolutionized the practice of European diplomacy because most of the work involves the sort

Table 3.1. Staff in permanent representations (1958–2000)

	1958	1968	1978	1988	2000
Belgium	6	17	24	27	53
France	5	19	26	28	89
Germany	5	28	41	42	87
Ireland	—	—	22	24	35
Italy	5	23	27	36	62
Luxembourg	1	3	2	2	13
The Netherlands	5	19	20	24	50
Denmark	—	—	26	32	47
United Kingdom	—	—	—	40	56
Greece	—	—	—	59	62
Portugal	—	—	—	37	49
Spain	—	—	—	32	63
Austria	—	—	—	—	41
Finland	—	—	—	—	51
Sweden	—	—	—	—	66

Source: Kassim and Peters (2001: 332).

of bargaining, management, and coordination that is typical of domestic politics.

Observers of the diplomatic scene argue that we are witnessing an integration of European diplomats (Hocking and Spence 2002). The tight timetable of EU summitry has put European diplomats in constant contact with each other. The need to coordinate a very wide spectrum of transgovernmental policymaking has forced foreign ministries to post diplomats permanently in Brussels. It has meant both that diplomats were integrating the EU element in their professional activity and that diplomatic practices were converging around EU rules. The functioning of the EU becomes an integral part of every national foreign policy. This has forced foreign ministries to adapt their policy focus, staff deployment, and administrative structures. For example, foreign ministries had to create *ex nihilo* the positions of political director (when, as was often the case, they did not have one), European correspondents, and CFSP units. But also, every geographical or functional unit had to task one of their officials to be the EU's "point of contact." Markus Ekengren (2002) has showed how the EU altered even the temporality of decision-making in foreign ministries and the writing styles, work habits, and vocabulary of their officials.

BUILDING THE EU AS AN INTERNATIONAL ACTOR: THE EXTERNAL DIMENSION

While the core of the EU's machinery is focused on so-called Community competences, such as the internal market, competition or agriculture, these are not the policy areas where diplomats exert the most influence nowadays. In fact, there is agreement that, as integration unfolded, most Community files were taken over by experts from specialized ministries. As a result, it is estimated that 70–80% of the staff in Permanent Representations are not career diplomats but "domestic" civil servants.[1]

One area, however, in which diplomats remain the dominant actors is the EU's foreign policy. To remain key EU actors, diplomats have had to go against their primary instinct, which was to keep foreign policy a national prerogative, and expand the scope of European foreign policy cooperation. In so doing, they laid the groundwork of a fairly constraining Brussels-based system of governance (Smith 2004). To paraphrase Alan Milward (1992), the following section is about the "European rescue of national foreign policy."

European Political Cooperation

The EU's foreign policy began in 1970, when foreign ministers from the Community launched European Political Cooperation (EPC). Fleshed out in the Luxembourg Report, EPC was meant to facilitate consultation and the exchange of information, with a view to coordinating if not harmonizing positions in the area of foreign policy. EPC was not based on strong institutions or commitments. Aiming for a limited number of meetings of foreign ministers (who were supposed to meet first twice and soon four times a year as a "Conference of Foreign Ministers of the EEC countries"), it was seen as a process to foster interaction between foreign policy actors more than as a binding arrangement between governments. As Hazel Smith (2002: 68) writes, "the specific aims of foreign policy cooperation between the six member states were cautious in the extreme."

---

[1] Email correspondence with the French, German, and UK Permanent Representations, Brussels, 2002.

Nevertheless, the first meeting, held in Munich, resulted in EU governments agreeing to participate in a coordination mechanism that *could* produce foreign policy outputs in the name of Europe. This in itself was new. Until then, there had been a great deal of diplomatic activity around shaping the EU and Community policies, but every proposal to give the EU a "voice" in the world had failed. The project of a European Political Community to oversee the European Defence Community had vanished when the latter was rejected by the French National Assembly in 1954. The Fouchet plan of 1961, which aimed at increasing coordination among the six founding members of the Common Market, was rejected by Atlanticist countries, notably the Netherlands, on the grounds that the proposed framework would be dominated by French interests and lead Europe away from Washington (Bodenheimer 1967).

EPC was kept rigourously separate from Community institutions, in large part because Paris did not trust the Commission (Nuttall 1992). It took place between capitals, and mostly at an official level. Two groups of officials formed the administrative backbone of EPC. Both groups consisted of diplomats from EU member states. At a senior level, political directors met at least four times a year, not in Brussels but in the capital of the country holding the rotating six-month presidency, to exchange views and draft the common declarations that would be issued by EU foreign ministers. This Political Committee (PoCo), as it was known, had no permanent home. Before 1987, when a small EPC secretariat was established, the preparation of meetings was entrusted to the rotating EPC presidency. In comparison to COREPER, the PoCo became legendary for its club-like atmosphere, which facilitated frank discussions with no expectation of result.

At a junior level, a group of European Correspondents was created to take on the routine aspects of EPC and prepare the work of the Political Committee. Also located in the foreign ministries, European Correspondents interacted with each other through a secure communications network created in 1973 and named COREU, for *Correspondance Européenne*. Through COREU, the exchange of telexes became multilateral: each message could be shared with the whole EPC community almost in real time.

For the most part, although it did produce a number of political declarations, EPC remained a talking shop (Ginsberg 1989; Nuttall 1992). As Simon Nuttall (1992: 12) quipped, EPC operated "by talking incessantly."

Occasional successes can be identified, as with the launching of the Conference on Security and Cooperation in Europe (CSCE) and with regards to South Africa, but they did not catch a lot of media attention. While EPC is not credited with a great number of foreign policy actions, it did, however, encourage a "coordination reflex" among European foreign ministries.[2] To some extent, the coordination reflex was aided by the gradual introduction of the notion that working procedures should be codified in a *coutumier*, while foreign policy declarations should be archived in a so-called *recueil*. Both were maintained by Belgium. The effects of this formalization of discussions began to be felt only slowly, but it became a sort of *acquis politique*, parallel to the *acquis communautaire*, the body of EU law that every member state, old or new, must abide to.

Notwithstanding the paucity of policy outcomes, EPC had two important consequences for European diplomats. First, interaction between foreign ministries increased more than was expected. PoCo meetings were held rather more frequently than initially envisaged. This led to a sharp increase in communication between foreign ministries: between 1974 and 1994, the number of COREU telexes rose from an average of 4,800 a year to more than 12,000 a year (Smith 2004: 101). According to one estimate, COREU exchanged around the turn of the century "in excess of 25,000 communications per year" (Spence 2002: 30).

This interaction was much enhanced by the creation of working groups, which brought together diplomats working on a wide range of substantive issues not specifically related to the EU, such as geographical (e.g. the Middle East) or functional issues (e.g. disarmament). These transgovernmental policy networks were responsible for developing, when possible, a European perspective on all the areas their foreign ministries were involved in. They still exist today and can make recommendations (in so-called "oral reports") to senior officials, for example political directors, for action. This expansion of European foreign policy beyond EU affairs meant than an increasing number of European diplomats had to meet in a specifically European context (Glarbo 1999). This was also a novelty.

The interpenetration of foreign ministries went further than simply exchanging views regularly. After 1977, foreign ministries began to lend

---

[2] This "coordination reflex" was already noted and prescribed in the 1973 Copenhagen Report, which comprised an annex documenting the EPC's output since its inception three years before (cf. Nuttall 1992).

some of their diplomats to the current EPC presidency, as a way to facilitate the work of a new mechanism, the Troika, which, comprising the past, current, and upcoming presidency, was meant to ensure the continuity of EPC's work. This efficiency requirement led to the current practice of exchanging policy officers between foreign ministries for quite extended periods of time.[3] Today, it is not uncommon for a junior diplomat to be seconded to the foreign ministry of another EU country.[4]

Finally, European embassies to third countries developed the habit of meeting and consulting each other on issues pertaining to EPC. Often the embassy of the EU presidency would deliver a joint *démarche* to local authorities.[5] This dense interaction was strengthened by the decision in the 1970s to coordinate EU positions in international organizations, notably the UN General Assembly (UNGA). Today, as a result of more than 1,000 internal coordination meetings per year, EU member states cast the same vote in UNGA 75–80% of the time. This is huge change from only 20 years ago. Consensus in the 1970s and 1980s oscillated between 40% and 50% of the time.[6]

EPC also allowed foreign ministries to take ownership of a project, European integration, that many diplomats feared would be cannibalized by economic actors. "The Political Committee," writes Michael E. Smith (2004: 78), "rapidly became a driving force behind EPC... [which] generally allowed foreign ministries (particularly the Political Directors) to play a much stronger role, although perhaps indirectly, in European affairs than before, after having been marginalized by other domestic ministries involved in EU business." For example, it was the PoCo that drafted the political provisions of the Single European Act and the Treaty on European Union.

The CFSP

Long a discreet process with no formal connection to Brussels, EPC was brought into the remit of the EU only in 1987, when its existence was finally acknowledged in the Single European Act. This treaty was "single"

---

[3] Interview, Ministère des Affaires étrangères, Paris, 2002.
[4] Interview, Ministère des Affaires étrangères, Paris, 2002.
[5] Smith (2004: 53) evaluates the number of common EU demarches to hundreds per year.
[6] Ernst Sucharipa's calculations quoted in Regelsberger and Wessels (2007).

precisely because it unified Community and EPC provisions. The UK was initially opposed to diluting EPC's "purity" but it eventually relented to avoid being embarrassed by the South African boycott issue (Budden 2002). As a first consequence of this "EU-ization," a small secretariat of approximately five seconded diplomats and their support staff was established in Brussels. EPC foreign ministers' meeting also began to be held back to back with EU foreign ministers' meetings (also known as the General Affairs Council), which put an end to the schizophrenic practice of holding distinct meetings in different cities with exactly the same individuals. These two small changes meant that EPC positions could now really be said to be made in the name of Europe.

This evolution culminated in the 1993 Maastricht Treaty, when the CFSP was instated as one of the three pillars of the EU, along with Community policy and Justice and Home Affairs. Although still intergovernmental, the creation of CFSP brought about a qualitative leap forward both in terms of instruments and organization.

In terms of legal instruments, the Maastricht Treaty added the possibility of joint actions, funded with Community budget, and strengthened the binding nature of political declarations with the institutionalization of common positions. According to Elfriede Regelsberger and Wolfgang Wessels (2007), the EU currently generates around 20–30 common positions, around the same number of joint actions, and close to 200 declarations a year—a sharp rise from 15 years ago. Both remain subject to unanimity in the Council, even though constructive abstention is now possible. In 1998, the EU added another instrument, the common strategy, which makes it possible for member states to use QMV on a common position if the common strategy was voted unanimously. This provision, I hasten to add, has almost never been used.

In organizational terms, the EPC Secretariat was fully integrated in the EU Council General Secretariat, whose staff was significantly expanded. When pertinent, EPC and Community working groups were merged (the Commission, having its own external relations policy in areas like development, humanitarian aid, and trade, relied on a distinct network of working groups, similarly involving national experts and often covering the same geographical issues). While the Political Committee remained in place for a while, it was now formally under the authority of COREPER. For all intents and purposes, the PoCo has now been replaced by the COPS, which is permanently based in Brussels and meets far more frequently than its predecessor.

A final important step came in 1999, when former NATO Secretary General Javier Solana was appointed to the new office of High Representative for CFSP. In addition to being double-hatted also being Secretary General of the EU Council, which gives him control over the entire Brussels-based intergovernmental machinery, Solana has at his disposal a Policy Unit, which undertakes early warning and prepares policy options—in other words, it gives Brussels its own capacity for foreign policy analysis.

The result of these changes has been a Brussels-ization of European foreign policy. Regelsberger and Wessels (2007) discern what they call a "ratchet effect," whereby national diplomats are increasingly involved in Brussels activities, which in turn means a "shift of political attention and personal resources to the Brussels arena." By Brussels-ization is meant an increase of the level of interaction among national experts around EU issues and often taking place in the European capital (Checkel 2005). The growth of policy output, the deepening of social interaction, the formalization of procedures, and the centralization of institutions that we have seen in this section all give credence to the Brussels-ization thesis.

On the one hand, Brussels-ization means that the EU's foreign policy remains an intergovernmental issue. It does not equate Communitarization, whereby competence over foreign policy would be transferred to the Commission, the Parliament, and the Court of Justice. Although the Commission is consulted and has a say over a number of issues, the decision-making process remains under the control of member states. The Commission has a limited right of initiative. The European Parliament's oversight is by and large restricted to the modest common budget, and the European Court of Justice has no authority to enforce supposedly binding commitments. In spite of the addition of common strategies, QMV is almost unheard of.

Yet, on the other hand, the most striking development since 1993 has been the integration of the *acquis politique* of EPC in the EU institutional framework. This has created strong linkages between EU policy and the EU's *foreign* policy. Indeed, Brussels-ization has meant a considerable increase in the organizational capacity of the Council Secretariat. The creation of the Policy Unit, the expansion of directorates-general concerned with foreign policy, and later the setting up of bodies dealing with security affairs, have brought the number of Council *fonctionnaires* to several hundred, about 200 of which work on CFSP files.[7] Most of these officials work on the coordination of working group meetings, which every week bring hundreds of national experts to Brussels. Virtually all CFSP meetings now take place in Brussels. Most of them, in fact, involve national experts who are based in their Permanent Representations.

In sum, much has changed between the early 1970s, when nine political directors, aided by their European correspondents, would meet perhaps every two months in Bonn or Paris to prepare biannual foreign ministers meetings, and the post-Maastricht period. The EU's foreign policy now involves hundreds of EU *fonctionnaires*, Brussels-based Permanent Representatives, COPS ambassadors, and CFSP counsellors, and probably more than a thousand diplomats, covering Latin America or airspace, who congregate in Brussels every few months to meet in *Justius Lipsus*, the Council Secretariat's building on Rond-Point Schuman.

In 1996, Christopher Hill and William Wallace (1996: 12) wrote that the "rising intensity of interaction" among foreign ministers and their officials had "further disaggregated the external solidarity of the state." Describing what they called an "engrenage" effect, they added:

Officials with less than twenty years' experience of national diplomatic services have grown up entirely within the context of European Political Cooperation, taking as given the exchange of confidential information not only about third countries but about their own governments' intentions and domestic constraints, the sharing of tasks (and sometimes facilities) in third countries, the acceptance of officials on secondment to their home ministry as no longer "foreign" but as colleagues.

This, it is worth noting, was written before e-mail, which has multiplied opportunities for direct interaction exponentially.

THE EUROPEAN FOREIGN POLICY FIELD

From 1970 to 1993, Michael E. Smith argues, European foreign policy went from being an intergovernmental forum to a practice of

---

[7] Interview, Council Secretariat, Brussels, 2005.

information-sharing to a formalized set of norms and organizations and to, finally, the basis of a system of governance. By governance he means "the authority to make, implement, and enforce rules" in foreign policy matters (Smith 2004: 176).

In the conceptual framework adopted here, European foreign policy has become a transgovernmental field. A distinct group of actors, consisting of hundreds of diplomats from the 27 member states, interact around a set of issues that they see as important. They vie for influence over the institutional architecture of the EU and the content of the EU's foreign policy. These actors promote different views and are endowed with unequal resources to promote these views. This section describes the characteristics of this European foreign policy field.

Actors

The actors of the European foreign policy field are mainly diplomats. Most foreign ministries comprise two divisions that deal with the EU: one that addresses Community issues and the other that focuses on political affairs (Hocking and Spence 2002). Typically, the Community division will work closely with other domestic government departments, such as economics or transportation, with which it will coordinate national positions on issues of Community competence. This is part of what I have called "shaping EU policy." In France, for example, the European cooperation directorate is one of the many government bodies that work with the General Secretariat for European Affairs (formerly SGCI), the central coordinating agency. The structure is similar in the UK, where the EU department (formerly European Community Department Internal) interacts with the Cabinet Office European Secretariat. In Germany, where the economics department plays a pivotal role, the *Europaabteilung* was nearly swallowed by the chancellery under Helmut Kohl but in the end remained part of the foreign ministry.[8]

The CFSP division will normally constitute a separate unit. Its task is to prepare a national position on the EU's foreign policy. The CFSP division is headed by the European Correspondent. As such, it has always maintained

---

[8] I thank Stephanie Hofmann who brought my attention to this peculiarity of the German decision-making structure.

close connections to the political affairs branch, under whose authority it was established during the days of EPC. Governments are organizing this relationship in different ways. In France and Germany, the CFSP unit is still part of the political directorate, while in the UK, the CFSP unit has been moved closer to their Community affairs colleagues under a common European branch. With the creation of ESDP in the late 1990s, another set of actors has begun to deal with the EU's foreign policy: namely the security and defence branch of foreign ministries and defence ministries themselves.

While these two or three divisions constitute the core of each country's capital-based European foreign policy actors, they are supplemented by colleagues from across the ministry's organizational chart. These colleagues meet fairly regularly in one of the EU's 30 working groups (out of 250) devoted to foreign policy issues. Issues discussed may include political developments in Venezuela or nonproliferation efforts in Korea. The European Commission, which has access to substantial budgets for its External Relations (Relex) and Development directorates-general, is an important player in these discussions. In addition, ambassadors to third countries and their staff, including from the Commission, meet as frequently as once a week to discuss and coordinate their action on the ground.

In Brussels, diplomats are particularly well represented in the political affairs and external relations sections of the Permanent Representations. There are teams to prepare COREPER and COPS meetings, as well as several officials to coordinate and attend the hundreds of working group meetings. Each Representation now also accommodates a substantial group of diplomats with political–military expertise. Much as environment ministries had to adapt to European integration, there is little doubt that foreign ministries had to adapt their structures and procedures as a result of European security and defence cooperation (Figure 3.1).

Social Representations

Cross (2006) argues that European diplomats have become part of an epistemic community, a network of knowledge-based experts who share causal beliefs and normative commitments. She shows that members of the

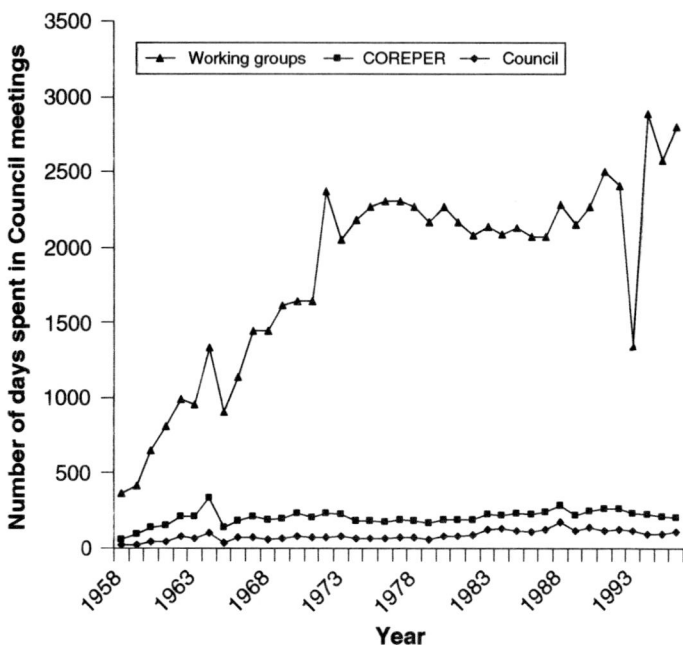

Figure 3.1. Meeting frequency: Council of Ministers, COREPER, and Working Groups, 1958–96.

Source: Kassim (2001: 20).

corps diplomatique tend to have similar social backgrounds, training, and professional status. In other words, the European *corps diplomatique* has a very strong *esprit de corps*. What the Europeanization of foreign policy has done is to increase considerably the frequency of their interaction. This in turn means that European diplomats are likely to share what she calls "professional norms." For Cross, the presence of these norms grants diplomats some autonomy from their governments and facilitates international negotiation.

Smith (2004: 122) makes a similar argument when he explains that the European foreign policy field is characterized by three explicit norms of behaviour: confidentiality, consensus, and consultation. Although criticized for deepening the democratic deficit, confidentiality is one of the norms most prized by diplomats and foreign ministers. Epitomized by Gymnich-type meetings, where foreign ministers meet without briefing notes or note-takers to discuss upcoming agenda items, the practice of confidential meetings is actually quite common down the hierarchical ladder (Nuttall 1992: 15). In the area of foreign policy, as in many others, most decisions are precooked by officials during business lunches or in the corridors.

Despite treaty battles around which countries should get how many votes in the Council, consensus-seeking is also a common practice in "everyday EU decision-making" (Lewis 2003). It is agreed that common positions cannot be forced down the throat of an EU member state. "There is, writes Meyer (2006: 124), a strong orientation towards reaching a common consensus." Finally, the "coordination reflex" means that consultation among EU partners is a daily habit (Glarbo 1999). It has been one of the objectives of CFSP since the beginning that EU governments do not make foreign policy decisions without first consulting with other EU governments. With a few notable exceptions, this coordination reflex has been internalized in the foreign policy practices of national actors, whether in the capitals, in the UN, or on the ground. The expression itself has become fashionable: it was a recurring theme during the interviews I conducted, when diplomats were asked what makes the EU different from other international organizations.

To these explicit norms Smith (2004: 122) adds two implicit ones: the prohibition against hard bargaining and the notion of *domaine réservé*. The former simply reinforces Cross's point that diplomats are more amenable to compromise than their masters would be; this *habitus* is encouraged early on in the diplomatic career, starting with recruitment (Neumann 2005; Meyer 2006: 124ff). The latter brings in an aspect of the European foreign policy field that we have not yet discussed: power, which I will take up in the next section.

While the makers of European foreign policy adhere to a common set of norms and even social dispositions, it is important to note that not all social representations are shared.

First, there are clearly a number of cleavages on substantive issues. These cleavages pertain in part to how the European foreign policy field should be ruled. British and French diplomats, for example, have long stuck to the view that foreign policy decisions should be arrived at unanimously, and with as little Commission input as possible. In interviews, they will refer to the fact that both the UK and France are nuclear powers with seats on the UN Security Council, which gives them "special responsibilities." Conversely, diplomats steeped in a federal culture that has privileged civilian power, like the Germans and the Belgians, are more comfortable with the notion of Communitarizing the decision-making process by involving the Commission and the Parliament, and increasing the use of QMV.[9] In addition, diplomatic actors do not always agree on the content of the EU's foreign policy. European divisions over the US intervention in Iraq were an extreme example of a long series of debates that have pitted proponents of "civilian power Europe" against advocates of "Europe puissance," and Atlanticists against Europeanists.

Second, as Roy Ginsberg (2001) noted, there exists a cleavage between those who have been socialized in the corridors of the EU's Community politics, and have come to carry a "culture of integration," and those who come from the political affairs tradition, are concerned with high politics, and favour a "culture of intergovernmental cooperation." In one ministry, the latter will literally refer to the former as "the other floor." EPC and the CFSP have been shaped by diplomats who believe that governments should remain in control of the foreign policy process. But the *rapprochement* of Community policy and foreign policy bodies since 1993 has meant that these individuals now have to deal with groups, both inside foreign ministries and outside, like in the European Parliament or the Commission, who support a greater degree of supranationality.

Power Structures

Power considerations play out in the European foreign policy field in two ways. First, there is obviously a struggle between EU governments for whose ideas will dominate the EU's agenda. Power asymmetries will often mean that big states get what their officials want. Whether on Community policies or during Intergovernmental Conferences, representatives from France, Germany, and the UK will usually set the agenda and hold a fairly credible veto power on initiatives they deem contrary to their interests (Hoffmann 1995; Moravcsik 1998).

---

[9] Interviews: Ministère des Affaires étrangères, Paris, 2002; Foreign and Commonwealth Office, London, 2002; Auswärtiges Amt, Berlin, 2002.

In the area of foreign policy, however, no government can really be coerced into doing something it does not like. The unanimity requirement gives a special role to diplomats, whose skills in framing arguments, building coalitions, and delivering results will impact on their government's influence. For example, Italy's relative lack of influence on EU affairs has often been blamed on its poor administrative capacity. Nevertheless, it is clear that CFSP output is hampered by the fact that the 27 governments constitute so many veto points. In that sense, the European foreign policy field is structurally more equal than other fields where decision-making if formally ruled by QMV. To counteract this egalitarianism, big member states are sometimes tempted to create *directoires* (Gegout 2002; Everts et al. 2004). The French, Germans, and British have developed a habit of working closely together so as to not get bogged down in the EU's slow decision-making process. They can then present the General Affairs Council with a *fait accompli* that the EU can either endorse or be left out of. ESDP and the so-called EU3's negotiations with Iran on nuclear nonproliferation are good examples of this.

Another way in which power shapes the European foreign policy field resides in the practices of the *corps diplomatique* vis-à-vis other professional groups. As I noted earlier, diplomats have been keen to promote foreign policy cooperation as a way to protect their turf against the encroachment of specialized ministries. While most EU policies have been "domesticated," European foreign policy is the only competence that remains truly theirs. While European integration means that diplomats are, in the words of a French official, being "dispossessed,"[10] it is also true that, the more the EU deals with high politics (whether in the form of treaty change or in CFSP), the larger the scope for foreign ministries' involvement. Diplomats may not always like Brussels, but they play the game well. Analysing the British case, Forster and Blair (2002: 98) thus write that "the growing influence of the FCO in the IGC process and the increasing frequency of IGCs represent a means by which the FCO can bolster a diminishing role in routine policy making in Whitehall." Together with CFSP, treaty negotiations remain a *domaine réservé* for diplomats, who deal directly with their own executive branch and foreign counterparts.

---

[10] Interview, Ministère de Affaires étrangères, Paris, 2002.

In that sense, one could say that the main stake of the European foreign policy field is to define the EU itself. Shaping EU institutions and controlling their access becomes a way to accumulate political capital. This explains diplomats' attachment to the development of CFSP. Without the Second Pillar, foreign ministries would have been almost entirely dislodged from Brussels. While foreign ministries still more or less control COREPER,[11] economic and financial affairs are led by economics ministries; justice and home affairs are in the hands of interior ministries; and environmental policy is decided by environment ministries. Supposedly the *primus inter pares* of Council formations, the General Affairs Council (foreign ministers), has seen its role decrease compared to the ECOFIN and JHA councils. Diplomats have only been able to remain important actors in the EU because they assist heads of state or government during summits and because CFSP has been put on top of the EU's agenda.

In other words, high politics have enabled diplomats to continue to see themselves as the EU's "elite." The idea that diplomats constitute a sort of state nobility is not new (Bourdieu 1989; Cohen, Dezalay, and Marchetti 2007). They were intimately associated to the construction of national states. On the basis of a highly valued form of cultural capital, shaped by attending select schools, fluency in several languages, social versatility, and a cosmopolitan ethos, diplomats claim an exclusive right to speak on behalf of the state. Perhaps more than the state's domestic elite studied by Bourdieu, diplomats have been key agents in shaping the reality of the state of which they are supposed to be the emissaries. Their professional practice is historically associated to the formation of the Westphalian state system. The sharp boundaries and legal foundations of national sovereignty were a prerequisite for the conduct of modern diplomacy, which in turn contributed to defining the national state.

And yet it is diplomats who built the European house. Formally, they still occupy key positions in the intergovernmental bureaucracy. In that regard, it is puzzling that most scholarly attention has been devoted to the role and ethos of Commission officials when, in fact, national officials

---

[11] There are actually two versions of COREPER. COREPER I is attended by deputy Permanent Representatives and deals with internal issues. COREPER II is attended by the Permanent Representatives themselves and deals with external issues.

such as Permanent Representatives have had as great if not a greater role in transcending the national state.[12]

CONCLUSION

To intents and purposes, European diplomats now operate in a strongly institutionalized EU environment, which the creation of a European External Action Service, confirmed in the 2007 reform treaty, should only serve to strengthen. Whether they deal with files that are internal to the EU or global in outlook, they must know and factor in the games that are taking place in the European foreign policy field. No resolution in the UN or national sanction on a third country can be issued without it having been first discussed with EU partners. By and large, European diplomats share a common understanding of what the rules and norms of this field are. These rules and norms specify how they should behave with their interlocutors, socially and institutionally; they become social dispositions. The fact that these rules and norms are defined in Brussels, where diplomatic interaction is denser than in any other city of the world, suggests that, for Europeans, the practice of diplomacy has changed considerably since the end of World War II.

It does not follow that contestation is absent from the European foreign policy field. On the contrary, the field is structured around struggles to shape the EU's foreign policy and impose one's definition of the EU. The practice of European diplomacy is about defining the "principles of vision and division" that will dominate the common European house. Social representations are shared but also diverse, and diplomats remain unequally endowed to promote theirs.

The Europeanization of foreign policy contains both a promise and a threat. The promise is that, by constructing a larger field of interaction, diplomats can hope that they will enhance their position vis-à-vis other specialized ministries that have also raced to Brussels since the creation of the EU. If they succeed in imposing their views to the EU, they can also use

---

[12] On Commission officials, see Georgakakis and de Lassalle (2007); Hooghe (2002); and Joana and Smith (2002). On Permanent Representatives, see Lewis (2003); and Menon (2004).

the strength of 27 member states to multiply their country's influence in world affairs. This promise corresponds to Hocking's "boundary-spanner" image.

The threat is that Europeanization will proceed in a way that diplomats or their political masters do not like, and thus that they will be imposed what they see as alien conceptions. The rules of the foreign policy field will then no longer be seen as adequate by key players. In this ever too likely scenario, diplomats would be tempted to retreat to national postures, enacting Hocking's "gatekeeper" image in a protectionist sense, or propose new ways of organizing the field. Such rethinking has often been forced by external events, which Stanley Hoffmann calls "terrible clarifiers." They are the subject of the next chapter.

4

European Security in Crisis

For West European countries, the end of the Cold War heralded the demise of the Atlantic regime described by Stanley Hoffmann (1995: 120) as "Atlantic-centred, United States-protected, and New York-financed." The two issues that had structured the European security environment since 1945, namely the Soviet threat and the German question, disappeared in a matter of months. No one really knew what would come after the dismantling of the Warsaw Pact (Niblett and Wallace 2001). Only one thing was certain: Lord Ismay's dictum that NATO was created to "keep the Soviets out, the Americans in, and the Germans down" no longer seemed an appropriate description of Europe's security challenges. While some believed that this would soon lead to a renationalization of foreign policies, others foresaw the emergence of a European superstate (Mearsheimer 1990; Siedentop 2002).

Beneath these grand geopolitical debates, foreign and defence policy-makers soon faced challenges of a different nature. Events seemed to conspire against European military and diplomatic institutions. The collapse of the East–West divide meant that the European continent was losing much of its interest for the superpowers, above all the US; it also deprived European armed forces of their *raison d'être*. Globalization seemed to undermine the importance of diplomacy as new actors played an growing role in a more complex, more interdependent environment. An economic downturn exerted strong fiscal pressures on the welfare state, whose security functions paled in comparison to strong demands for health, education, and pension programmes. Finally, the war in the Balkans signalled a resurgence of conflict in Europe, which no country was ready to address.

All of these events, which took place in the early 1990s, precipitated the international defence and the European foreign policy fields into crisis. In the conceptual language adopted in the Introduction, they suffered "external shocks." These shocks severely affected the military and diplomatic institutions, notably by reducing their budgets and legitimacy, but also by threatening the way in which these two institutions had organized themselves on an international level for the past 40 years. In this chapter, I describe what the effect of these external shocks was, and how certain actors sought to propose different solutions to the crises, all of which revolved around reconfiguring the links between the European foreign policy and the international defence fields.

PEACE DIVIDENDS AND THE DOWNSIZING
OF EUROPEAN ARMED FORCES

The fall of the Berlin Wall brought the idea of "peace dividends." It was hoped that a new and more peaceful international order would make large and expensively equipped armed forces redundant. This normative pressure on defence budgets was compounded by the fact that European countries faced simultaneous fiscal and economic crises in the early 1990s. Budgetary orthodoxy held sway, partly as a result of Thatcherite economics in Britain, partly as a result of the single currency's Maastricht criteria in France and Germany. In the latter country, the costs of reunification and economic stagnation worsened the crisis. In this difficult context, military expenditures were sacrificed at the altar of more pressing welfare state priorities (see Figures 4.1 to 4.3).

Between 1987 and 1991, defence expenditures as a percentage of gross domestic product (GDP) fell from 4% to 2.8% in France, from 3% to 1.9% in Germany, and from 4.7% to 4.2% in the UK. While defence expenditures in Europe oscillated between 5% and 7% of GDP in the mid-1960s, they had dropped to between 1.4% and 2.3% around the turn of the twenty-first century. These budget cuts led to an important restructuring of European armed forces. Between 1987 and 2001, military personnel declined by 50% in France and 38% in Germany. In the UK, regular forces declined by one-third. In these three countries, defence ministries launched large-scale downsizing and modernization drives. They proceeded at different speeds, with the UK, which had already dealt away with the conscription burden, going the fastest, while Germany trailed behind considerably.

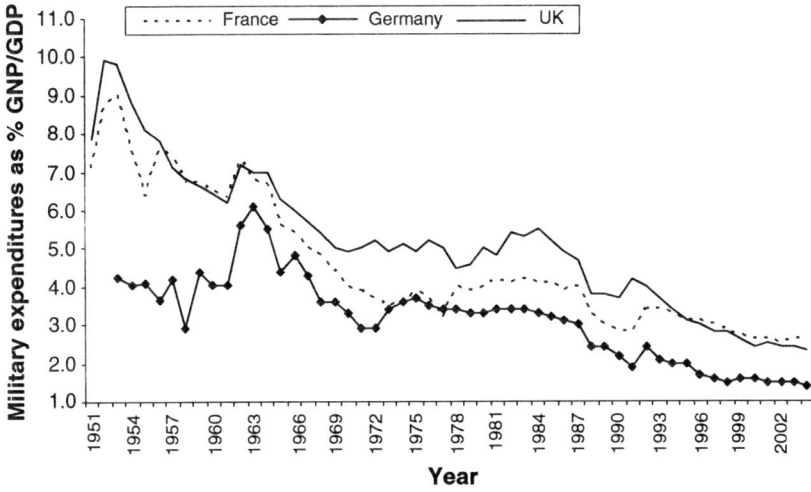

Figure 4.1. Military expenditures as a percentage of GDP: France, Germany, and the UK (1951–2004).

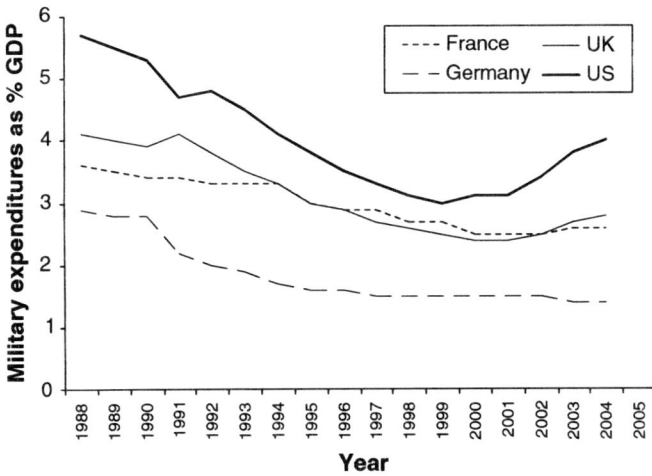

Figure 4.2. Military expenditures as a percentage of GDP: France, Germany, the UK, and the US (1988–2005).

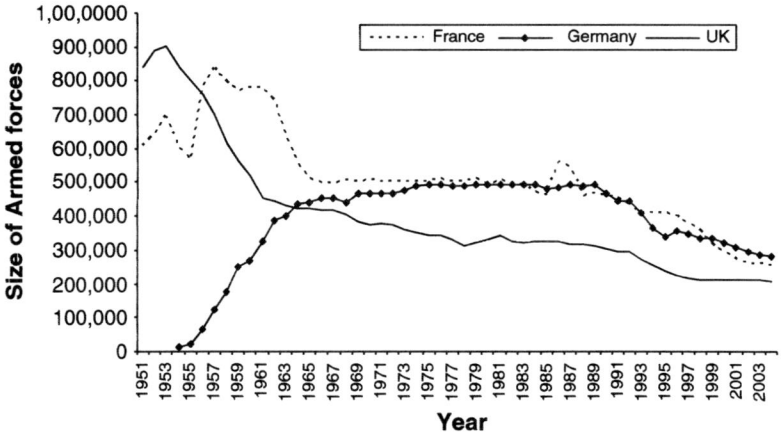

Figure 4.3. Military personnel: France, Germany, and the UK (1951–2004).

Source: Military Balance, International Institute for Strategic Studies, various years.

The modernization of British services culminated in 1998 with the *Strategic Defence Review*, which aimed at strengthening "jointery" and "projectability," and extended the privatization of auxiliary services to help focus on core tasks. In practical terms, the objectives of jointery and projectability were met with the creation of a Permanent Joint Headquarters, a Joint Rapid Reaction Force, and a Joint Services Command and Staff College.

The UK at least had the advantage of a 30-year-old all-volunteer force tradition. Reform in France, where national service was part of the social and political fabric of the republican state, would prove much more difficult. The first Gulf War had shown that French military capabilities were neither exhaustive nor interoperable in a high-intensity conflict. Conscription in particular had proved to be an operational liability. France was able to send only 15,000 troops in the Persian Gulf (Thomas 2000: 37). The 1996 reform aimed at enhancing projection capabilities at the relative expense of nuclear forces, which were the basis of France's defence posture since the 1960s. Armed forces were restructured to make them more cost-effective given the declining importance of the European theatre. Several units were dismantled, and the remaining ones were assigned to multinational operations in ever increasing numbers (Gautier 1999). As in the UK, a Joint Staff (EMIA) and a Joint Staff College were created. Most importantly, the reform aimed at doing away with conscription, which weighed on projectability, by 2002. As Bastien Irondelle (2003*a*: 208) writes, the reform was nothing short of a "revolution, in which the complete professionalization of the armed forces and the abolition of conscription were the fundamental modifications."

In even worse shape was the German *Bundeswehr*. Even after having integrated the *Nationale Volksarmee* from East Germany, *Bundeswehr* personnel was slashed by one-third from its peak years during the Cold War; this meant a total cut of almost 50% (Duffield 1998: 144). In contrast to the UK and France, which had always maintained an expeditionary component, the German force structure was entirely based on territorial defence. Armed forces were forbidden constitutionally from sending combat units abroad. A first positive step towards force projection was taken in 1994 when the Federal Court in Karlsruhe ruled that the *Bundeswehr* could be deployed outside the NATO area in an allied context. This was the beginning of the end of Germany's "culture of reticence," (*Kultur der Zurückhaltung*), which eventually led it, by the early twenty-first century, to become one of the biggest troop contributors to international operations, notably in Afghanistan, the Congo, and Lebanon.

While the citizen–soldier paradigm remained a political taboo preventing the abolition of conscription, the number of conscripts was reduced and professional elements given greater emphasis (Sauder 1995). Slowly, more power was given to the General Inspector (the chief of the defence staff) in the conduct of military deployments. A Joint Operations Command (*Einsatzführungskommando*) was created in Potsdam (Baumann 2001). The Germans, who in a series of half-baked reforms tried to build up strike forces (*Einsatzkräfte*), were first baptized by fire in Bosnia, but their force structure, heavily reliant on conscription and armour, and with few units at a high level of readiness, was considered ill-fitted for these new times (Meiers 2001; Sarotte 2001).

Europe's military resources, both economic and human, were dwindling fast. But the procurement picture was even bleaker. In 2001, for example, the US purchased US$60 billion of new equipment while the three European powers spent just US$16 billion (Keohane 2002: 7). The US spent US$40 billion on defence-related R&D while France, Germany, and the

UK combined spent US$7 billion. Between 1987 and 1998, military R&D spending, *in absolute numbers*, fell by 38% in France, 26% in Germany, and 27% in the UK.

The downsizing of procurement programmes caused alarm among military staffs, especially since the modern, smaller, deployable armies that they were asked to create rely considerably on expensive technology. They feared what Bernard Boëne (2003: 170) calls "structural disarmament," which he describes as follows: "As budgets cannot possibly catch up with spiralling investment costs, the number of big-ticket items bought to equip the armed services is lower with each generation of weapons. There will, for instance, be fewer *Leclerc* main battle tanks or *Rafale* aircraft than there were *AMX* or *Mirage* previously in the French army."

In sum, the 1990s saw a change in Europe towards leaner, more flexible, more professional, and much poorer armed forces. Defence ministries experimented with a variety of organizational designs. In each country, the force structure was modified so as to facilitate the "modularization" of units—for example, at the battalion level—that could then be used as the building blocks of ad hoc force packages, in a more flexible way and for a greater variety of missions. This was an important change compared to the previous model, based on large armoured divisions of little use in light, expeditionary warfare (Dandeker and Freedman 2002). Part of the reason for these changes was that the pre-1989 defence posture had been "rendered obsolete" (Unterseher 1999). But equally important was the fact that armed forces were, budgetarily speaking, no longer sacrosanct.

In particular, force structures were modified to reflect diminishing resources and mounting political pressures to "go overseas." In the 1990s, every NATO summit focused on means to attain these two objectives. While the 1991 *Strategic Concept* stuck to the primacy of collective defence, it also highlighted the necessity of simultaneously shrinking the Alliance's force posture and making it available to the UN for global security and peace missions. As soon as 1993, American pundits began to argue that NATO had to "go out of area or go out of business": the alliance had to be ready and willing to extend its reach towards Eastern Europe (Asmus, Kugler, and Larrabee 1993). In addition to enlarging NATO's membership, this meant that NATO had to refurbish itself for crisis management missions outside Western Europe: non-Article 5 operations, so called because they do not involve collective defence issues but threats to international security more generally.

Expanding the geographical scope of the Alliance proved to be not too much of a problem. It was fully endorsed in the 1999 new *Strategic Concept*, which focused on both enlargement and new missions. But the transformation of NATO forces remained—and has remained to this day—a preoccupation. At the 1999 Washington Summit, the Allies launched the Defence Capacity Initiative, which aimed at fostering the "mobility," "deployability," and "sustainability" of their forces for out-of-area operations. Facing the Initiative's obvious failure in improving Europe's balance sheet, NATO endorsed in 2002 the Prague Capabilities Commitment, which identifies and seeks to address key capability gaps through more focused measures. The Prague Commitment is part of a broader, US-imposed transformation of the Atlantic Alliance, which also includes the reorganization of command structures and the creation of a 17,000-strong NATO Response Force. In principle, defence ministries have come to accept that improving Europe's military capabilities will require that armed forces cooperate more with each other, share a greater number of assets and capabilities, divide labour according to their "role specialization," and coordinate their procurement programmes. While small countries like the Netherlands or the Czech Republic adapted to these changes quite well, for example, by investing in operational niches such as special forces or biowarfare, bigger states find it hard to accept that they will not be able to retain the full spectrum of capabilities.

Clearly, the end of the Cold War and the US Congress's threat to disengage from NATO pushed European countries to reshape their armed forces. With new missions, much of their force structure became obsolete. Operations in the 1990s, writes a military expert, "revealed the widening gap between the capabilities of the US, and those of its European allies; the increasing inapplicability of NATO's Cold War war-fighting doctrine to operations like Bosnia an Kosovo; the growing divergence between European doctrines and emerging US concepts; and the Allies' collective failure to prepare adequately for coalitions" (Thomas 2000: 56). With more than 1 million enlisted personnel, EU countries could hardly deploy 60,000 troops abroad. Europe trailed the US in the so-called revolution in military affairs, with its heavy emphasis on costly high technology. The Pentagon was no longer interested to "interoperate" with European forces that could not keep up with their technological prowess.

Throughout the 1990s, this "capability gap" constituted the main preoccupation of European defence planners. David Yost (2003: 93) summarizes the reasons why the gap matters: "Americans resent European 'dependents' telling the United States how to run Alliance operations, while Europeans resent dependence on US capabilities." This fear of European forces losing their ability to deploy with the US is encapsulated in a catchy phrase, often heard in Brussels: European soldiers do not want to wash the dishes after the Americans have done the cooking. This is very much how coalition operations in the Balkans and later in Afghanistan were perceived by the Europeans.

Thus, the crisis of the international defence field was twofold. It was first a crisis of *legitimacy*. The European military was deprived of its enemy. It had to look for a new *raison d'être*, which was found in international peace support operations. These new missions required that defence ministries invest in force projection. To a greater or lesser extent, all European armed forces modified their force structure to emphasize force projection, professionalize their troops, and, in many cases, abolish conscription. This is what should allow them to participate in multinational operations. To some extent, they had succeeded by the turn of the twenty-first century. As Andrew Dorman (2002: 17) writes, "there is a steadily expanding manpower pool within Europe available for use in expeditionary warfare, even though the overall European military manpower pool is diminishing."

But they had to do this with much reduced resources, for the crisis was also a *budgetary* one. This context made it difficult to afford duplicating your neighbours' assets. Despite its integrated military structure, NATO procedures did not give strong enough of an impetus to divide the labour among European armed forces. Again, this led to a strategy of internationalization, which the European label helped to sell to governments, parliaments, and the public (Irondelle 2003*a*; Posen 2006). The development of operational niches like the Czechs' biowarfare units, the establishment of a European Airlift Centre, the Europeanization of defence firms like EADS, and the purchase of equipment "off the shelf" are probably only the first steps in a radical rationalization of the military field in Europe.

MISSING THE HOUR OF EUROPE

Soon after the signing of the Maastricht Treaty, which coined the CFSP, Christopher Hill (1993: 306) lamented that there remained a "capabilities-expectations gap." Europe's foreign policy, he argued, had been "talked up." In spite of its economic weight, the EU did not have access to the basic legal, political, diplomatic, and military capabilities that would enable it to fulfill internal and external demands.

This sombre assessment was given confirmation in the Balkans, where the disintegration of Yugoslavia dealt a blow to the EU's foreign policy aspirations. Between 1991 and 1993, the EU was actually quite active, in effect taking over "leadership of the mediation efforts" (Ginsberg 2001: 58). "The hour of Europe has dawned," exclaimed Jacques Poos, Luxembourg's foreign minister. But this hyperactivity could not conceal deep divisions among member states. These divisions were uncovered early, when the German government engaged in unilateral action by recognizing the breakaway provinces of Slovenia and Croatia against the will of French and British diplomats. They continued as London and Paris expressed their willingness to put their soldiers in harm's way, while Bonn (and Washington) appeared much more reluctant. As the crisis escalated into all-out war, European divisions led to paralysis. A series of EU-brokered peace plans failed. Serbia's uncompromising attitude further underscored the impotence of the common foreign policy. "The Union," writes Adrian Treacher (2004: 56), "had evidently ceased to act as a single entity in the crisis."

As a result, the EU was soon out of the picture and replaced in 1994 by the Contact Group, comprised of the UK, France, Germany, Russia, and the US. With the UN Protection Force, France and Britain had troops on the ground, but France's efforts to bring in the WEU, which would have acted with a much stronger mandate in the name of the EU, failed. In the face of spiralling violence, the UN agreed in 1994 to let NATO (i.e. the US) launch air strikes. In the event, NATO replaced UNPROFOR the following year to implement the Dayton peace accords signed in November 1995 under the patronage of the US.

Bosnia may have been, in Ginsberg's words, European diplomacy's "baptism by fire," but it was widely considered as an inauspicious one. In Bosnia, as later in Kosovo, Europe's management seemed disastrous because it was incapable to act united, alone and, even if it could agree, did not have the means to do so. Timothy Garton Ash (2005: 108) puts it quite eloquently:

Europe "screwed it up" all right. While EU representatives made endless diplomatic efforts to halt the bloodshed, and while EU national governments argued among themselves, more than 200,000 Europeans, among them many unarmed civilians, women and children, were brutally murdered by other Europeans. At least 3 million people were driven out of their homes. This was bad old Europe, as it had not been seen since 1945.

The Balkans wars illustrated vividly the "capabilities-expectations gap." Declaratory diplomacy, the main output of the European foreign policy field, had failed. Without military capabilities, Europe had to satisfy itself with being the proverbial "political dwarf," reliant on US power for any meaningful action. Jean-Yves Haine (2001: 99) argues that "primary victims of Europe's military impotence, French and British diplomacies drew similar lessons from the Bosnia crisis, the first of which being the necessity for Europe to implement a defence policy that would allow it to become genuinely autonomous." While this analysis somewhat anticipates future developments that were far from certain at the time, there is no doubt that one lesson was drawn: without Washington, European foreign policy was tragically ineffective. For the British, this meant that every effort should be made to "keep the Americans in." For the French, this meant that Europe had to ready itself to act autonomously.

The European foreign policy field was thus subject to a twofold crisis. On the one hand, the "shifting pattern of world politics" accelerated the decline of national foreign policies, at least European ones (Hocking 2002: 1). In the 1960s or 1970s, squeezed between the superpowers but on prime terrain and with privileged links to their former colonies, French or British diplomats could hope to punch above their weight (Risse-Kappen 1995). This prospect seemed unlikely in the post-Cold War world. Faced with the continuous domestication of EU policy, which deepened after 1993 with the launch of the single currency and the development of Justice and Home Affairs, diplomats had to find solace in the further Europeanization of foreign policy. The CFSP could, in principle, generate "politics of scale" and put Europe centre stage again (Ginsberg 1989). But *démarches* and sanctions were of little use in the face of a real, violent conflict. When the going got hard, and required military capabilities, European foreign policy had to give way to NATO and the US.

A NEW SECURITY ARCHITECTURE

The European security landscape of the mid-1990s was populated by a host of "interlocking institutions" which made up the continent's complex "security governance" (Croft 2000; Webber et al. 2004). The CSCE was trying to build on a large membership and a history of confidence-building measures to foster a sense of cooperative security "from Vancouver to Vladivostok." The EU was stabilizing the continent by extending its institutions to Central and Eastern Europe. NATO clearly remained the most credible military alliance, as it had shown in Bosnia. Its European pillar, the WEU, seemed for a while to be a promising one, insofar as it could be transformed into the EU's "military arm."

The "Byzantine complexity" of interlocking security institutions, however, did little to solve the crises which European diplomats and soldiers were experiencing (Andréani, Bertram, and Grant 2001: 39). To address these, many institutional solutions were offered, all of which proposed to redefine the relations between security institutions and reshape the European security environment. Stuart Croft identifies four of these "narratives"—here I focus on only three, the fourth one being a short-lived Russian creation. The first narrative was the transformation of the CSCE into a powerful security community, a sort of bridge between the EU and the UN. The second was the militarization of the WEU, which in the end would create a "Europe of Defence." The last option was the Europeanization of NATO.

Cooperative Security in Europe: The CSCE

The Conference (now Organization) on Security and Cooperation in Europe was created in August 1975 by the US, Canada, the Soviet

Union, and all of the European countries except Albania. The objective of the drafters of the Helsinki Final Act was to establish a system of cooperative security. The conference was construed as a normative framework, supported by annual meetings, to foster negotiated agreements in the area of confidence-building measures, disarmament, the peaceful resolution of disputes, human rights, terrorism, and environmental issues. The idea was to create an arena where security problems could be discussed between the two opposing camps. Neutral and pacifist governments were particularly keen to see the development of a demilitarized security community that would focus on international socialization, confidence-building, the spread of peaceful norms, and so on (Adler 1998; Thomas 2001).

After 1989, Chancellor Kohl and Hans-Dietrich Genscher, his foreign minister, promoted the CSCE as a pan-European security framework that included the USSR as well as the US. Consistent with Bonn's *Zivilmacht* culture, the conference placed Germany at the centre of the security environment while simultaneously furthering its diplomatic focus on soft mechanisms of confidence and cooperation building (Duffield 1998). The 1990 Paris Summit seemed to herald a great future for the CSCE. Annual meetings of a Council of Foreign Ministers were instated; a permanent secretariat and a Conflict Prevention Centre were created in Prague and Vienna. The institutionalization of this framework was illustrated in 1995 when the Conference became an "Organization."

Bonn's hopes that the CSCE could provide a credible vehicle to implement security arrangements were dashed in the Balkans, where the belief that soft security organizations based on confidence building measures could prevent conflicts from arising was fatefully put to the test. As a way of organizing the European security environment, the CSCE never recovered from its painful Balkans experience. Embroiled in internal conflicts with Russia about democratization, it slowly disappeared from the regular agenda of French and British foreign ministers.

A "Europe of Defence": The WEU

Starting in 1954 as an intergovernmental European security organization based on the its predecessor, the Western Union, to facilitate the integration of Germany in NATO, the WEU had since the mid-1980s, when first President Mitterrand and then Jacques Chirac tried to "relaunch" it, acquired an intriguing dual dependency: on the one hand, it remained the "European pillar" of NATO in Europe but, on the other, it became symbolically invested with the emerging security activities of the EU. This reflected a fundamental opposition between the three military powers of the EU. While Great Britain wished the WEU to remain intergovernmental and under full NATO control, Germany wanted to "communitarize" the WEU within the structures of the EU while retaining a strong but independent link with NATO. France, for its part, would have rather kept the functioning of the WEU autonomous from both NATO and the EU, thus retaining its intergovernmental but distinctively European character (Dumoulin and Remacle 1998; Rees 1998).

In reality, only French diplomats really believed in the WEU, which they saw as a way to give Europe a credible form of military autonomy. This belief must be understood as part of the Gallic narrative on the "Europe of Defence." To give substance to this narrative, the French launched a number of political initiatives in the defence field. They often received the ambivalent support of German politicians and diplomats. Together, they created the Franco-German brigade in 1988 and then, joined by Belgium, Spain, and Luxembourg, the Eurocorps in 1995. In 1996, two multinational forces were created with Italy, Spain, and Portugal: the EUROFOR, a rapid deployment force with a permanent headquarters, and EUROMAR-FOR, a nonstanding maritime force.

Following the June 1992 Declaration of Petersberg, which stated that the military units of WEU member states could be used to prevent conflicts or manage crises in out-of-area, low-intensity zones—including terrorism, humanitarian catastrophies, and even ecological disasters—these forces, along with NATO's ACE Rapid Reaction Force, were made available to the WEU for specific operations and called "Forces Answerable to WEU" (FAWEU). To support this new philosophy, WEU structures were strengthened with the setting up of a smallish military staff, a Situation Centre, and a satellite-interpretation centre in Torrejon. The WEU conducted a limited number of small operations in the Adriatic and on the Danube. But its action, kept deliberately symbolic and never fully embraced by German and British officials, was overshadowed by NATO.

Europeanizing the Alliance

The integrated military structures of the Alliance have been at the heart of French complaints since their creation in 1950 because they are de facto headed by an American general. Mounting frustration led President de Gaulle to withdraw French forces from these structures in 1966. Since then, Europeanizing the Alliance has always been a French condition for its full return.

As a response to the strengthening of the WEU, Allied leaders came to support the creation of the US-inspired concept of Combined Joint Task Forces (CJTF). This flexible means of organizing command and control within NATO would, it was hoped, give life to what came to be called the European security and defence identity. These multinational force packages were "separable but not separate" from the NATO integrated structure and could be requested by the WEU for European, non-Allied military purposes. NATO European officers would formally switch to the WEU, and Deputy SACEUR, a European general, would take command. The North Atlantic Council, however, had to give its assent to the use of these "collective assets" of the Alliance (Schake 2002; Terriff 2003).

The *rapprochement* of the WEU and NATO gained some momentum when Jacques Chirac became President of France in 1995. France's foreign minister announced that his country would rejoin NATO's Military Committee and promised that full reintegration would be given consideration if NATO agreed to Europeanize its structures, notably command posts. "By the mid-1990s," writes Charles Cogan (2001: 83), "the French had begun to shift tactics. Rather than trying to create a separate European identity around the WEU, with all that implied in terms of cost and redundancy of effort, ... the French announced their readiness to create a distinctively European defence 'pillar' within NATO."

These developments were celebrated at the Berlin Summit in 1996. The creation of CJTFs, with their attendant lending of NATO assets to the WEU, and the Europeanization of NATO's military structures became the doctrinal core of ESDI. The idea was that Europe could not afford duplicating NATO assets. But Europe could be given a greater say within the Alliance, and even act alone when the US was disinclined to join (Sloan 2002). This in effect meant the burial of the French idea of a "Europe of Defence." For Stuart Croft (2000: 8), the Europeanization of the Alliance marked "the victory of the Anglo-American idea."

Yet, the ESDI model collapsed for two reasons. First, Paris halted its *rapprochement* with NATO when its request that a European officer be put in command of Mediterranean Forces in Naples was rejected by the US. This was taken by the French as an indication that Europeanizing NATO from within was impossible. Second, and more profoundly, the WEU, which was supposed to lead European efforts when the US declined to participate, proved too weak a political institution. Unknown to the public and dormant for many decades, the WEU did not have the necessary legitimacy to request and direct substantial NATO forces. As a French official reportedly asked, the CJTF concept "looks as though it will work in practice, but will it work in theory?" (quoted in Sloan 2002: 100). The WEU's relationship with the EU was also quite tenuous and remained debated. As three foreign policy experts wrote, the London- (then Brussels-) based organization "lacked the clout, the critical mass, or the political visibility which could command respect from individuals, states, or organizations (neither the EU nor NATO ever condescended to treating the WEU seriously, though the EU and NATO do treat each other with respect)" (Andréani, Bertram, and Grant 2001: 39).

RESHAPING FOREIGN POLICY AND DEFENCE IN EUROPE

Let us briefly analyse these events in the light of political sociology. The properties of a field, like the European foreign policy field or the international defence field, are always contentious. In his work, Bourdieu emphasized time and again that, despite their reproductive logic, fields are also arenas of conflict where knowing and playing with the rules of the game (*ars inveniendi*) is crucial. What Fligstein calls "social skills" enable an actor to induce cooperation among other actors for his or her own purposes through framing the issue in a way that resonates with these potential allies, or brokering between various interests. When conditions are relatively fluid or when the field is in crisis, socially skilled actors may be able to exploit the institutional vacuum and modify the rules of the field.

In Bourdieu's sociology, the organization of a field usually breaks down when an external shock occurs. As long as current arrangements seem to work to the benefit of the most important actors—or at least not to their detriment—serious challenges are unlikely. But if they are perceived as irrelevant or suboptimal, often as a consequence of drastic changes in the environment, other ways of structuring relations may be explored. This is precisely what happened with the end of the Cold War and the Balkan wars, which as we saw profoundly destabilized the international defence and European foreign policy fields.

External shocks create opportunities that socially skilled actors can utilize. The field is in flux as actors rethink their relations to each other. Coalitions become uncertain, power structures less clear, and actors are looking for new ways to play the game around changing stakes. Individuals like Genscher, Kohl's foreign minister, or collective actors like French diplomats tried to use the perceived diplomatic and military crises to promote their ideas. These state actors mobilized their political capital as well as that of others by creating coalitions on the basis of issue-specific common interests (e.g. addressing "intolerable massacres at the heart of Europe") or structural affinity (e.g. the objective challenge faced by European diplomats, whether in London or in Paris, which led them to favour similar options). To do that, it was necessary for these actors to be able to perceive what was at stake in both the foreign policy and the defence field, who the key actors were, and what was objectively feasible; in other words, they needed an intimate sense of the game and the field. In the language of international relations, the social skills involved in finding a solution acceptable to other key players is what we call "diplomacy."

But success was not guaranteed. Fluidity characterizes well the situation described in this chapter. The vast amount of political time expended in summits, conferences, declarations, communiqués, nonpapers, and op-ed pieces was focused on reshaping the European security environment. Clearly, there were geopolitical imperatives behind these grand architectural designs. But reshaping the European security environment was also intimately linked to more profound—and more concrete—preoccupations about the role of foreign and defence policy in the new Europe. It was about finding a new *raison d'être* for European armed forces in a context of diminishing resources; it was also about bolstering the role of European diplomats despite strong skepticism about their relevance.

There is not enough space here to recount the numerous initiatives that aimed at reshaping the European security environment. Predictably, they all more or less fell under one of the three narratives outlined above: cooperative security, the Europe of Defence, and a Europeanized Alliance. To some extent, all of them provided a coherent picture of how European security could be organized.

None of these, however, proved compelling enough to carry the day. This is partly because they proved relatively inefficient in terms of addressing security challenges; this at least could be said of the CSCE. But the main reason, I suggest, is that they all failed to resonate with or provide major incentives to at least one of the dominant sets of actors in the European foreign policy and the international defence field.

The cooperative security option, which built on the CSCE's tradition of "seminar diplomacy," did nothing to address the crisis in the international defence field. In fact, it more or less amounted to sidelining the military, whose role in solving crises was lessened. It is not surprising, then, that it was never taken seriously by Europe's two military powers, France and the UK. Somewhat similarly, the "Europe of Defence" promoted by the *Quai d'Orsay* was strongly resisted by Atlanticist countries, whose armed forces were tightly integrated in NATO's military structure. As Lord Robertson, Britain's defence secretary, said, "what frighten[ed] us is that it could put not very much in NATO's place."[1] Even in French *military* circles, the idea was given little more than lip service.[2]

Conversely, Europeanizing NATO, even if it had not been blocked by France for symbolic reasons, provided a very technical response, narrowly based on military cooperation, to what diplomats saw as a large political problem. As Giegerich (2006: 58) writes, ESDI was a "military–technical arrangement." Granting more command posts to the Europeans in the Alliance did not enhance the role of European diplomats. In fact, it could be argued that it threatened to undermine further the European foreign policy field. The WEU, whose role was promised to be strengthened, lacked political legitimacy. The conduct of security policy would have remained in NATO's hands, with little if any role for the EU's CFSP. This would have sapped the work of diplomats, even British ones.

In sum, these institutional blueprints resonated neither with broad social representations, like France's independence or Britain's Atlanticism,

---

[1] Interview with the author, London, 2005.
[2] Interview with senior officer, Ministère de la Défense nationale, Paris, 2002.

nor with the bureaucratic interests of defence and foreign policymakers. As I have argued elsewhere, state actors are socialized by their national and organizational environment, from which they derive deeply held beliefs about the role of the state, the nature of security challenges, and the purpose of their organization (e.g. the *Quai d'Orsay* or the *Bundeswehr*) (Mérand 2006). The proposed "narratives" contradicted too many of these worldviews. They also failed to placate the power structures entrenched in the European foreign policy and international defence fields. Either the military or diplomats stood to lose. As a result, these scenarios were not perceived as adequate responses to the crises experienced by Europe's diplomats and soldiers.

State actors, however, agreed on one point: reshaping the European security environment would necessitate rethinking the relations between the European foreign policy and the international defence field which, until then, had more or less existed alongside one another. The vague idea that some institutional overlapping would benefit Europe's security governance was gaining ground.

CONCLUSION

In this chapter, we have seen that, however strongly institutionalized they are—both NATO and EU foreign policy *were* strongly institutionalized by the early 1990s—fields can and do experience crises. "A crisis," writes Fligstein (2001*b*: 264), "implies that dominant actors in an institutional arena begin to lose out...Episodes of institution-building are framed by actors' perceptions of crisis and their ability to react to that crisis." In these moments of uncertainty, or fluidity, there is usually no shortage of "solutions," with political entrepreneurs to carry them. Eventually, new commitments, new symbols, new interests, new sets of relationships, and perhaps even new actors will arise in the process of reorganizing the field.

The question is, which and whose solution will prevail? Political science provides us with three different answers. For rational-choice theorists, government actors engage in utility-maximizing bargaining: within the constraints of their respective resources and barring any gridlock, they will devise a set of institutions that best serves their interests. For historical and sociological institutionalists, the future will be highly constrained by the past, either through the sedimentation of interests or the institutionalization of norms: the new solution will often be a case of either "layering" or "everything must change so that nothing changes." For constructivists finally, political entrepreneurs are likely to play a key role in mobilizing coalitions and reshaping the field around a normative focal point.

It is difficult to adjudicate between these explanations so long as a "solution" has not clearly won over its rivals. The period of crisis covered in this chapter, roughly from 1990 to 1997, did not see the unambiguous victory of any new (or old) conception. The European security landscape remained in flux. The fact that state actors had preferences, that there were political entrepreneurs around, and that there was plenty of negotiation going on did not suffice to make anyone's idea prevail. Despite their striking similarities and the fact that each of them was a significant improvement over the status quo, the three main solutions on offer failed. Although a period of *tâtonnement* is to be expected in times of reorganization, I have suggested that the failure of state actors to give a definitive new shape to European security had to do with structural and symbolic conditions that were not met by any of the advanced proposals.

In the Bourdieusian perspective adopted here, it is clear that, to reorganize a field, one cannot start from scratch. As I wrote in the Introduction, periods of stability are followed by periods of creativity and social action, but this creativity is always bounded by objective conditions. While the occurrence of an external shock matters tremendously and usually brings about a host of new institutional "solutions," there cannot be a total break with the practices of the past; emerging social representations must resonate with old ones; and more importantly, the vested interests of dominant actors must be taken into account. Viewed in this light, it is not entirely surprising that none of the "solutions" promoted to address the crisis of European security worked.

That is why it is important to open up the black box of institution-formation. Fields are not *ipso facto* reconfigured by a change in actors' preferences; nor can they be expected to simply carry on forever. In the next chapter, I explore the rise of the ESDP as an option that was only marginally different from the others, was also fiercely fought over by state actors, but has so far managed to pass the test of time. As we will see, the role of political entrepreneurs able to gauge the changing environment and the objective conditions they faced was crucial, as were contingent events over which they had little control but which they managed to use creatively.

5

Constructing European Defence

In the last chapter, I described a number of institutional blueprints that were put forward to address the challenges faced by European diplomats and defence actors while reshaping the European security environment. I argued that, because they failed to resonate with the social representations or to answer the interests of key actors in the international defence and European foreign policy fields, none of these initiatives carried the day.

One initiative, however, did eventually prove successful. Like the "Europe of Defence" and ESDI options presented in the last chapter, the European security and defence policy implied a certain *rapprochement* between NATO and the EU. But it also differed from its failed predecessors in a number of important ways. Unlike French proposals to transform the WEU into the defence arm of the EU, ESDP was portrayed as a bottom–up process, which would rationalize existing forms of cooperation, and eschew grand architectural designs *à la* common European defence. But unlike the British proposal to Europeanize the Atlantic Alliance, ESDP granted decision-making autonomy to the EU. In other words, ESDP promised to enhance the role of European foreign policymakers without undermining the cherished military infrastructure of defence planners.

That said, the future of ESDP was never scripted. As will become clear, the formation of a European security and defence field was a contingent and creative process. Presented from 1999 onwards as a means to help solve a Balkans crisis, it has become a multifaceted project that is used to intervene in the Congo, buttress civilian crisis management, and restructure Europe's defence sector, in addition to giving Europe "a voice in the world."

As Charles Grant (2002: 85) argues, politicians did not play a major role after they had set out the basic parameters of ESDP. "Much of the hard work of building ESDP, he adds, has fallen to senior officials, such as political directors and heads of policy in defence ministries." This chapter describes how the European security and defence policy was crafted by a relatively small but international group of state actors from foreign and defence ministries who were trying to tackle security architecture problems and were genuinely dedicated to making this work (Howorth 2003). These civilian officials held key positions in their respective organizations, they had been around for some time and sensed not only what their political masters expected but also what others could be expected to agree to. They also knew each other, and eventually went on to hold very prestigious posts in their profession—in other words, they had social skills.

These actors defended solutions that were in synch with their own interests and social representations, either national or organizational. As I argued elsewhere, when they utter the words "European defence policy," British officials will stress *policy*, the French will underscore *defence*, and the Germans will focus on *European* (Mérand 2006).

THE ST. MALO INITIATIVE

The launch of ESDP in the fall of 1998 was largely a by-product of British domestic politics and the EU diplomatic agenda. At the 1996–7 IGC, the British delegation was seen as defending rearguard positions. Tony Blair's Labour government was elected towards the end of the negotiations that led to the Amsterdam Treaty. The change of government allowed unforeseen progress on some EU files. Britain agreed to sign the Social Charter and lifted its opposition to the French idea of a High Representative for the CFSP. But its position on European defence remained firm: nothing labelled "EU" was to happen on this front.

As part of the UK presidency of the EU, which lasted from January to June 1998 and was considered a mixed bag, Tony Blair asked mandarins in several government departments for a review of the UK's European policy (Whitman 1999; Deighton 2001; White 2001: 137). Discussions were held in meetings of the Subcommittee on European Questions of the Defence and Overseas Policy Committee (Dover 2005: 514). Having opted out from Schengen and the euro, it was difficult for Britain to find its place, to use Blair's words, "at the heart of Europe." After borders and the single currency, and especially with the series of crises in the Balkans, diplomats felt that calls for a more European stance in the area of security and defence were inevitable, at least on the continent. As then secretary of defence George Robertson recalls, "We were convinced that, sooner or later, we would be ambushed at a next [EU] Summit."[1]

Robertson asked his staff to draft a memo for the Prime Minister. The note, written by civilian officials (and, importantly, not the defence staff), argued that Britain should come forward with a proposal that "would break the logjam."[2] Since the end of the Cold War, there had been no substantive progress on the European security architecture. Germany favoured a greater EU role, France defended a strengthening of the WEU, and Britain stayed put on NATO, eventually encompassing a European security and defence *identity*, but Europe as a whole seemed incapable of acting militarily, even when it wanted to.

It is perhaps not a coincidence that, at that very moment, senior officials and foreign policy experts were arguing in London that a move "towards a European capability to act independently in the defence field" could help Britain "lead in Europe." Roughly, the idea suggested by these individuals was to create a fourth pillar within the EU to deal with defence issues, on an intergovernmental and transatlantic basis, where British military assets would ensure leadership.[3] As Craig Parsons (2004) argues, new ideas often come stronger at the interface of partisan politics and intellectual struggles. It is hard to tell whether these ideas came from government officials or think tanks, but they certainly reinforced each other.

The British proposal was discussed first among British and French officials—the officials that I interviewed disagreed about whether MoD policy directors or diplomats took the lead. The German attitude was to let the French and the British sort out the details, as long as they were kept in the loop (Jopp 1999). At this stage, discussions were held among *civil* servants. "In fact, concedes Hubert Védrine, the former French Foreign Minister, I was informed fairly late in the process by my political director."[4]

---

[1] Interview with the author, London, 2005.
[2] Interview, Ministry of Defence, London, 2002.
[3] Papers by Robert Cooper, Senior FCO Diplomat, and Charles Grant, Director of the Centre for European Reform, a think tank close to Labour. See the *Economist* (10 October 1998) and *The Financial Times* (1–2 October 1998).
[4] Interview with the author, Paris, 2005.

After a few months of discussion, it was agreed that European defence would feature on the agenda of the Franco-British Summit to be held in St. Malo on 4 December 1998. This was made possible by the volte-face in the British Ministry of Defence. As Robert Dover (2005: 518) argues on the basis of interviews that are congruent with mine, Tony Blair had decided to press ahead as early as October 1998, "whilst the debate between the MoD and FCO concerning the policy [i.e. to what extent the EU should be given a security and defence role] remained unresolved." From the French perspective, the agenda item was an uncontroversial one, especially after their failure to Europeanize the NATO chain of command the preceding year. Perceiving a unique opportunity, Lord Robertson notes, "the French packed it up and ran away with it."[5]

Tony Blair began to make references to "Europe" and "defence" a few weeks before St. Malo. His change of tone was noticeable at the informal EU meeting held in Pörtschach in October 1998 and, in November, EU defence ministers were allowed to meet for the first time, albeit informally (Salmon and Shepherd 2003: 66). But, as Michael Quinlan (2001: 28) the former British MoD senior official notes, "The thinking-aloud character of the Pörtschach exchanges and the fact that meetings of this kind do not issue a communiqué meant . . . that the significance of these reflections . . . was not generally noticed, perhaps even among EU foreign and defence ministries and overseas missions." By December 1998, however, European defence was no longer the preserve of defence officials: it had become a matter of foreign policy, therefore the domain of diplomats who jumped on the wagon as soon as the competence became theirs. This was especially true in France, but even in Britain the FCO and the Cabinet Office were quick to take over from the MoD.

The Joint Declaration on European Defence adopted in St. Malo read:

The Union must have the capacity for autonomous action, backed up by credible military forces, the means to decide to use them, and a readiness to do so, in order to respond to international crises . . . Where the Alliance as a whole is not engaged, the Union must be given appropriate structures and a capacity for analysis of situations, sources of intelligence, and a capability for relevant strategic planning, without unnecessary duplication . . . In this regard the European Union will also

---

[5] Interview with the author, London, 2005.

need to have recourse to suitable military means (European capabilities pre-designated within NATO's European pillar or national or multination European means outside the NATO framework).[6]

In modern diplomatic language, the St. Malo Declaration is called a "deliverable." It is an agenda item that makes a high-level meeting appear successful. While deliverables are not devoid of content, they are prepared with particular expediency because they are driven by a timetable and a public relations agenda. It would appear that the somewhat less noted speech in Pörtschach, two months before St. Malo, responded to the same logic. As Dover (2005: 511) writes, the overtures at Pörtschach and St. Malo were announced "with a perception of undue haste, especially in the context of defence policy being seen to be a slowly evolving policy area."

The language in the declaration was discussed until late at night during the summit. The word "autonomous" was the most controversial: did it mean that Europe should develop an independent decision-making structure in the area of defence, as the French hoped for? Or did it simply mean that Europe should enhance its military capabilities, as the British insisted? One imagines that, following diplomatic custom, several words were "bracketed" until the last minute.[7] As Hunter and Farley (2002: 30) write, the "construction [of the St. Malo Declaration] permitted a wide range of interpretations, and those by British and French officials immediately began emphasizing quite different parts of the declaration." Once again, the use of "constructive ambiguity" (Stanley Hoffmann's term) allowed diplomats to conceal deep-seated oppositions and conclude a successful summit.

From the point of view of foreign ministries, the St. Malo Declaration was a great deliverable: it was taken up by the press and continues to be quoted today. For mostly ideological reasons, it is hard to imagine that a Conservative government would have seen it through; but the British government's eagerness to prove its European credentials was also a key factor. Brian Rathbun (2004) has argued that partisan politics was an important factor in the British volte-face: The launch of ESDP was contingent on a Labour victory. But it was also contingent on the need to find

---

[6] See *From St. Malo to Nice. European Defence: Core Documents*, ed. by Maartje Rutten. Paris: Western European Union Institute for Security Studies.

[7] Interview with a senior French diplomat, Paris, 2002.

a deliverable to conclude a successful summit, and the creativity shown by senior French and British officials in finding one. While Tony Blair did "cross the European defence Rubicon," (Howorth 2000a: 34) there was no distinguishable change of strategy that would have responded to a radically altered perception of the environment. As most observers noted, the European Defence Initiative was not terribly different in substance from ESDI. The French and the British were simply experimenting with ways to find a common ground which, despite the use of an ambiguous vocabulary, would appear to be a diplomatic success. There is little evidence that, at this stage, they sought more than this.

On the one hand, British officials clearly sought an expedient response to parochial problems: finding ways to assuage French demands for a more ambitious EU security policy, giving the new Labour government an area where it could display European leadership and, more pragmatically, finding a deliverable for an important Franco-British summit. On the other hand, the negotiations that preceded the declaration focused on finding wording that would resonate with both French and British traditional conceptions of security policy (Mérand 2006). Social skills were important in elaborating new ideas that would be "culturally" acceptable to both camps.

That being said, the European Defence Initiative launched an important process of institution-building. For, by then, the only thing that was clear was that Britain agreed to a greater EU role in defence, and also to the possibility of European operations outside the NATO context. St. Malo was a step forward in papering over social representations and authorizing officials to engage more deeply in reconfiguring the European security architecture. That was a conceptual breakthrough, but one which, like many others before, remained vague and could have soon fallen into oblivion. The institutional foundations needed to be buttressed before ESDP became what it is today. What, if anything, would a "greater EU role in security and defence" look like?

AN ESDP SHAPED AFTER NATO

The EU cycle of political initiative depends a great deal on the system of rotating 6-month presidencies. The country that took over the presidency immediately after the St. Malo Summit was Germany. Conceptually, the Cologne Summit Declaration and the German Presidency Report of June 1999 read like cut and paste versions of the St. Malo Declaration (Hunter and Farley 2002: 56).[8] Yet Berlin used its presidency to clarify and strengthen the conceptual breakthrough of St. Malo. At an informal meeting of foreign ministers in Reinhartshausen, in March 1999, German diplomats tabled a paper sketching out how the WEU should be merged with the EU in a "common European defence policy." The idea was fleshed out at a meeting of foreign and defence ministers later that month in Bonn. Gone were the ideas of a European security and defence identity within NATO, or a greater WEU role at the service of the EU: the notion was *entrenched* that the Union itself should have its own political–military structure.

The German presidency laid out the basic institutional architecture of what was not yet known as ESDP.[9] Their final report "brought a major change to the evolution of the [CFSP] and ESDP, making far-reaching proposals on institutional, policy, and capability enhancements" (Salmon and Shepherd 2003: 68). ESDP was clearly put under the second pillar of the EU (CFSP). Since the early 1990s, CFSP had been located in the EU Council Secretariat. This implied for ESDP that there would be a dominant role for the General Affairs Council, and a strengthening of the High Representative for CFSP and his Policy Unit. This implication was illustrated with great clarity by the appointment as High Representative of Javier Solana, a senior political figure with extensive international experience.

Berlin also sketched out the political–military organization chart. As the then Defence Minister Rudolf Scharping recalls, "We told the UK: go ahead with capabilities, we'll deal with institutional things."[10] At Helsinki, in December 1999, the EU confirmed the creation of three permanent political–military bodies in the Council: a committee of ambassadors with political–military expertise exercising political control and strategic direction (COPS); a military committee to provide military options

---

[8] Cologne European Council, 3–4 June 1999. See *From St. Malo to Nice. European Defence: Core Documents*, ed. by Maartje Rutten. Paris: Western European Union Institute for Security Studies.

[9] Interview with a senior German diplomat, Berlin, 2002.

[10] Interview with the author, Berlin, 2005.

(EUMC); and a military staff (EUMS). This structure was later formalized in an Annex to the 2001 Treaty of Nice.[11]

The institutional architecture that was devised in the course of 1999 did not constitute a revolution of the sort that President Chirac advocated, in a letter he sent to other EU leaders, with an autonomous chain of command and a multinational HQ. But it was more ambitious than the British had probably envisaged. European defence would be neither solely about the transatlantic relationship nor an instrument of European *puissance*; instead, it would have to serve, in Cogan's (2001) words, the "third option."

In fact, the ESDP structure is an amalgamation of two existing templates: NATO and the CFSP. This is perhaps not surprising, since successive German governments have been the most earnest proponents of the view that the Atlantic Alliance and the EU's foreign policy were perfectly compatible objectives (Dumoulin et al. 2003).

The political–military component is an exact replica of NATO's. The COPS is to the EU what the North Atlantic Council is to NATO. The membership of the EUMC overlaps to a large extent with that of NATO's own Military Committee. The EUMS is a smaller version of NATO's International Military Staff, where military officers were usually assigned prior to moving to the EU.[12] NATO was the model behind the creation of EU political–military bodies—with the notable exception of SHAPE, a full-scale operational headquarters which the EU lacks. The logic was impeccable and reassuring to defence staffs: if the EU was bound to use NATO assets for its operations, which most policymakers insisted they would, it made sense that its political–military structures mirrored those of NATO.[13] This hope was not shared by all, as French officials were reluctant to endanger the "integrity" of EU decision-making (Brenner 2002).

The political authority, for its part, is clearly derived from the CFSP pillar of the EU. The British idea to create a fourth pillar for security and defence was not adopted. And while the WEU was to be merged with the EU, its *modus operandi* was not: because of the reluctance of some foreign ministries, the choice was made not to draw explicit institutional

---

[11] See *From St. Malo to Nice. European Defence: Core Documents*, ed. by Maartje Rutten. Paris: Western European Union Institute for Security Studies.

[12] Interview with an EU Military Staff officer, 2002.

[13] Interview with a German official, Brussels, 2002. So-called "Berlin Plus" agreements were being negotiated to allow the EU to have access to NATO planning assets and capabilities. See Terriff (2003).

linkages with NATO, not to give a privileged status to non-EU NATO states and, more crucially, not to create a council of defence ministers.[14] Instead, political–military bodies follow CFSP rules and are located in the Council Secretariat, thus making of ESDP the direct legacy of the integration of EPC in the EU treaty at Maastricht, in 1993. ESDP was merged with the CFSP architecture, not put alongside it. This implies, *inter alia*, a potential role for the EU High Representative. This basic architecture would not change thereafter: 50 years of Political cooperation became, so to speak, part of the ESDP *acquis*.

In the choices that were made, one finds clear elements of path dependence (Pierson 1996). What makes this path dependence rather innovative is that *two* institutional structures were merged, leading not to institutional reproduction but to a whole new set of institutional arrangements. Strongly committed to both NATO and the EU, Berlin was in a unique entrepreneurial position to flesh out the ways in which the international defence and the European foreign policy fields would be combined. London and Paris had slightly different—and sometimes opposed—visions of how ESDP should operate. The transition from the decision to launch ESDP to the choice of its institutional framework was greatly facilitated by a skilful but accidental German presidency.

FRAMING KOSOVO: THE HELSINKI HEADLINE GOAL

At the same time as the basic institutional structure was put in place, thought was being given to the purpose of ESDP. European countries, notably France, have been toying with the idea of "common defence" at least since the 1950s. The objectives then ranged from defending the continent against the Soviet bloc to furthering European integration to creating a third force. But it is only in the late 1990s that European defence became a crisis-management tool and a means to restructure the defence industry rather than a step towards a European army.

In November 1999, for the first time, defence ministers were formally invited to attend the General Affairs Council. Britain ratified a Franco-German proposal to give the EU its own rapid reaction pool through the

---

[14] Interview, EU Council Secretariat, Brussels, 2002.

means of a capabilities objective: approved at the Helsinki Summit, this became the so-called "Headline Goal." The idea, laid out in the Finnish Presidency's *Progress Report on Strengthening the Common European Policy on Security and Defence* but most probably canvassed from French and especially British papers, was for the EU to have at its disposal the equivalent of an army corps of 60,000 troops, supported by air and naval elements, deployable within 60 days and sustainable for at least a year on the field (Quinlan 2001: 37; Menon 2003: 211). With that goal in mind, member states should set themselves a target to identify and fill capability gaps.

These numbers did not come out of nowhere. Headline Goal targets are precisely what the EU had lacked during NATO's intervention in Kosovo, which aimed at dislodging Serbian troops from the province's territory and, lasting from March to June 1999, was the century's last war on the European continent. The emphasis on specific capability gaps was the common denominator in two documents produced around that time by the UK and France, respectively: *Kosovo: Lessons from the Crisis* and *The Lessons of Kosovo*. The difficult experience of European governments in Kosovo, where they had had to rely extensively on US air strikes and thus follow US strategy, was interpreted as the kind of situation that ESDP would need to address in the future. Kosovo was used as an additional reason to strengthen ESDP; as a result, it became, for a while, the rationale of ESDP.[15] And yet, Kosovo was not the *cause* of ESDP. The project of European defence predated the Balkans wars. But this external event, which was in everybody's mind from 1997 to 1999, was both framed as a justification for ESDP and used as a frame to define what purpose ESDP should serve.

In a food-for-thought paper, British officials proposed that a Capabilities Commitment Conference be convened to help achieve the Headline Goal. The conference was held in November 2000. Member states made specific pledges towards a Force Catalogue. The following year, after a Dutch initiative, defence ministers agreed to put together a European Capability Action Plan to improve Europe's balance sheet in military equipment. Eighteen panels made up of military experts and chaired by different countries were set up to identify shortfalls and find solutions (Schmitt 2004). The impulse behind ECAP was to enable the EU to

---

[15] On the two conceptual meanings of "framing," see Goffman (1974); and Medrano (2003).

conduct a Kosovo-type operation with a rapid reaction force. The list of capability gaps and the force structure that ECAP produced stemmed from the Kosovo experience. ESDP became synonymous with strategic airlift (the A400M aircraft), sea transport, precision-guided munitions, and electronic warfare, namely the capabilities that European countries had lacked during the NATO operation (Quinlan 2001: 37; Clarke and Cornish 2002).

While the Headline Goal has had little expansionary impact on European capabilities so far, it allowed the Europeans to go beyond institutional debates and focus on something tangible. Defence experts provided the expertise and set the practical limits to what was initially a diplomatic process. They were able to move forward because they agreed on technical issues, making ESDP a bottom–up process. As François Heisbourg (2000: 80), the French defence analyst, writes, the Headline Goal was the "small detail" that sparked a debate on strategic objectives and the means to attain them. More importantly, it brought in defence staffs, which were steeped in a NATO culture and became increasingly involved in institutional debates. Thus began with ESDP the *démarche capacitaire* that had been absent in previous European projects.

Once governments had agreed to focus ESDP on the improvement of capabilities, it became difficult to resist the calls to Europeanize the defence industry that had grown increasingly vocal since the 1990s. Industrial competitiveness became a salient issue. The late 1990s saw a number of high-profile mergers in the EU defence sector, as well as increased awareness of the dominance of US firms. European governments sought to accompany these supply-side changes by launching demand-side initiatives, notably the 1996 Organization for Joint Armament Cooperation (OCCAR) and the 1998 Letter of Intent (Mörth 2004). The *démarche capacitaire* also allowed the Commission and the "Community method" through the backdoor. As we saw in Chapter 1, the European Commission had long criticized Article 296, which enables member-state governments to argue that the defence industry is a matter of national security and can be exempted from common market regulations (Keohane 2002). In September 2004, in yet another attempt to open up the defence procurement market, the Commission's DG Internal Market issued a Green Paper on Defence Equipment Procurement, which received a fairly wide media coverage, especially since it came after EU leaders had agreed to set up a European Defence Agency (Britz and Eriksson 2005: 49).

The European Defence Agency was one of the most consensual initiatives discussed during the European Convention. It was agreed in June 2003 to launch it before the Constitutional Treaty was even signed. Located in the Council, the EDA is steered by a board of defence ministers. This Steering Board, which resembles a defence formation of the Council of Ministers, is chaired by Javier Solana, and not, as is usually the case in the intergovernmental pillar, by the defence minister of the country holding the presidency. Moreover, the Board will function by QMV. The EDA associates the Commission to its work, since the Commission has the power to bring down trade and investment barriers, invest in research and technology, and promote industrial restructuring.

A defence agency working by QMV, chaired by an EU figure and involving the Commission is something one would have thought anathema in the world of EU foreign and defence policy. Headed by Nick Whitney, the former UK defence official, overseeing 80-odd military officers and civilian officials, the EDA has integrated most of the Headline Goal panels. The EDA's focus is on creating networks of defence procurement officials, defence staffs, and industrialists. In the area of capabilities, for example, "Integrated Development Teams" will associate Council Secretariat, Commission, and capital-based experts. A senior EDA official suggests that the EDA may be the tool that allows national defence staffs to take ownership of ESDP in Brussels itself.[16]

For a long time, European defence was seen as an ingredient of political integration in Germany, an element of *Europe puissance* in France, and an irritant in Britain. Framing it as a capability-enhancement process aimed at enabling Europe to prevent crises on the continent, as in the Balkans, took ESDP beyond past controversies. It gave a new rationale to an old idea like European defence.

REDEFINING THE HEADLINE GOAL FOR AFRICA

As Kosovo vanished from the headlines, French and British diplomats turned their attention more firmly to Sub-Saharan Africa. There had already been joint diplomatic initiatives in Africa in the 1990s. In St. Malo,

---

[16] Interview with the author, Brussels, 2005.

Tony Blair and Jacques Chirac had mentioned the possibility of bilateral efforts in the area of African security. France and the UK share in this region similar interests and approaches but they are both encumbered by their colonial past: in addition to bringing considerable humanitarian and development resources, the EU could bring a multilateral legitimacy that each country lacks individually (Faria 2004).

Then, in May 2000, the UK intervened in Sierra Leone. Beginning in 2002, France became involved militarily in Côte d'Ivoire. African security was squarely back on the agenda. At around the same time, New York and Brussels were intensifying their dialogue on how the EU could better contribute to UN peacekeeping efforts. In August 2003, at the request of UN Secretary General Kofi Annan, France led an operation in the Democratic Republic of Congo: Operation Artemis. An opportunity was seized to bring the EU on-board. Although the German defence ministry initially resisted the idea of a French-led EU operation in Africa, political reasoning prevailed in Berlin and the EU Council eventually gave the go-ahead.[17] The French expanded their joint operations centre to integrate European staff officers. Troops from the UK, Germany, Belgium, and Sweden joined Operation Artemis. Although led by the French, all decisions and documents (concepts of operations, etc.) had to be seen by the EUMS and the EUMC, and vetted by the COPS.[18] This was the first "autonomous" EU operation, that is, the first operation conducted without recourse to NATO assets.

Operation Artemis in the Congo was made possible because thinking in London and Paris on the value-added of ESDP for Africa was already quite advanced. After Sierra Leone, discussions between London and Paris on the possibility that France and the UK could unite their efforts in Africa had intensified.[19] At the Franco-British Summit of Le Touquet, in February 2003, leaders openly mentioned their plans to prepare for autonomous EU crisis management operations in Africa. The development of ESDP appeared as a means to legitimize the engagement of Paris and London on the African continent in that it offered the prospect of replacing the *tricolore* and the Union Jack by the EU flag. These discussions also came at a convenient time when Britain and France were otherwise at odds over

[17] Interview with a senior EU Council Secretariat official, Brussels, 2005.
[18] Interview with an EU Military Staff officer, Brussels, 2005.
[19] Interview with a senior British diplomat, London, 2002.

Iraq: a joint EU initiative seemed opportune to mend their rift. Europe also entered the equation of defence ministries which began to see ESDP as a means to strengthen their defence diplomacy programmes and get access to EU funding (Bagayoko 2005*a*). Currently, the UK and especially France are going out of their way to promote the "Europeanization" and "African ownership" of their African defence policies. "We hope," a British diplomat told me, "that we will never have to deploy on our own in the future."[20]

The EU operation in the Congo substantially altered the objectives of ESDP. Although declarations continued to mention it, the dominant template would no longer be the Kosovo-inspired Headline Goal for a heavy rapid reaction force of 60,000 troops, but a package of smaller, more mobile, combined and joint units which, like Operation Artemis, could move in a theatre quickly, stay for two months, and then withdraw as other stakeholders, such as the UN, take over. This became the "battle group" concept, an idea, launched by Britain and France, that was approved by foreign and defence ministers in May 2004. The force structure underlying ESDP was reconfigured to incorporate the new concept of "force packages" then gaining prominence in the French and British defence staffs (Dandeker and Freedman 2002).[21]

Battle groups are self-sufficient, 1,500-strong joint units that can be deployed in 15 days and sustained for at least 30 days in a theatre of operation. Under the new "Headline Goal 2010," 15 battle groups will be established. Big states will form their own while smaller states are expected to join their efforts in multinational groups, making the battle group an illustration of permanent structured cooperation in an EU context. Each group will have a lead nation and an associated headquarters. In theory, an EU battle group can be dispatched quickly but it is expected that the AU or the UN will take over after a while.

Simultaneously, ESDP was added to the toolbox of instruments that can be mobilized to strengthen EU policy towards Africa. The emergence of a strong EU–AU relationship since 2003 occurred at a time when the international community, notably the G8, was increasingly getting involved in supporting African peacekeeping capabilities. While the Commission was setting up an African Peace Facility to bolster such efforts,

---

[20] Interview, Foreign and Commonwealth Office, London, 2002

[21] Interview with a French defence official, Paris, 2006.

the political–military structures of the EU Council sought to both support and intervene in Africa.[22] This has opened up channels of communication between the Commission and the Council—an interesting case of "cross-pillarization." New organizational units have emerged, such as the so-called Crisis Action Teams, which are meant to coordinate the EU's civilian and military efforts. But the probability of conflict between the two Brussels institutions has also increased.[23]

The new African focus of ESDP does not follow straight from the St. Malo initiative: developments that are external to ESDP, in and around Africa, had to be seized upon by diplomats, originally more with the aim of strengthening ESDP rather than buttressing the EU's African policy. The idea was not originally developed in African desks but in security desks responsible for ESDP.[24] External developments were interpreted and framed as a way to expand the scope and demonstrate the value of ESDP. An "ESDP for Africa" was seen both as a means to legitimize ESDP and an interesting new tool to address rising security challenges in Sub-Saharan Africa. In the words of Niagalé Bagayoko, the Congo mission in particular was seen as a "testing ground" (*terrain d'expérimentation*) for ESDP (Bagayoko 2005*a*; Gegout 2005).

In sum, the "African turn" has had a substantial impact on the scope, purpose, and institutional arrangements of ESDP. It has shifted the geographical focus, modified the privileged force structure, and introduced new actors in the policy domain, such as the Commission's DG Development. Without an ESDP already in place, the EU would not consider military intervention in Africa; yet, it is important to emphasize that the EU would probably not have created an ESDP solely for that purpose either.

Initiated to address the 10-year-old stalemate over the architecture of European security, the geographical mandate of ESDP expanded in 5 years from Kosovo-type operations to supporting the EU's African interests. While the EU is now leading an important operation in Bosnia, where

---

[22] Interviews, Council Secretariat and European Commission, Brussels, 2005. See also Faria 2004.

[23] In November 2003, the EU approved the creation of a Peace Facility for Africa, which provides for the use of EU money to support African-led crisis management operations and African Union planning capabilities. Since then, the AU and the EU have been in a close "peace and security" dialogue, especially on Darfur (Faria 2004).

[24] Interviews, Foreign and Commonwealth Office, London, 2002, and Council Secretariat, Brussels, 2005.

an EU Force has replaced NATO's SFOR, forward planning is clearly on a different brand of mission.[25] The rapid reaction force associated with the Helsinki Headline Goal is still in the books, but focus has shifted on battle groups, which fit particularly well with the emerging EU strategy of supporting AU efforts in the area of crisis management.

CONSTITUTIONAL EFFERVESCENCE AROUND EUROPEAN DEFENCE

On 29 April 2003, in the midst of the Iraq War, French, German, Belgian, and Luxembourg leaders met in Brussels. They proposed the creation of a European Union of Security and Defence (EUSD). Following the model of the Economic and Monetary Union, the four leaders argued that the EU should enable structured cooperation in defence based on "convergence criteria," a mutual defence pact, expanded Petersberg tasks, a European Defence College, and a European Defence Agency. The "chocolate summit," named after a staple of these four countries, was widely seen as controversial because it also proposed that an EU military headquarters be set up in Tervuren (a location suggested by the Belgian Prime Minister). The British immediately opposed this proposal, which they saw as an attempt to duplicate SHAPE and decouple ESDP from NATO. Yet, as Howorth (2004: 488) writes:

Over the course of summer 2003, both sides moved towards one another. British enthusiasm for developing military capacity, for early warning systems, for appropriate planning facilities (including the strengthening of HQ capacity), for a defence agency and other military objectives were all entirely compatible with the main EUSD proposals.

At a trilateral meeting in Berlin, in September of that year, Britain agreed with France and Germany, on the basis of a British food-for-thought paper, that an autonomous EU planning cell could be set up provided that it not be located in Tervuren and links be tightened with NATO planning structures. British conditions were symbolic. The *location* of Tervuren was problematic only because it was too closely associated with the Franco-German initiative; and EU–NATO links were already very close

---

[25] Interview with an EU Council Secretariat official, Brussels, 2005.

thanks to Berlin Plus arrangements, which provide for the lending of NATO's planning and operational capabilities to the EU (De Schoutheete 2004: 41).

The other effect of the chocolate summit was to highlight the work being done in the Defence Working Group of the European Convention, then in full swing. The group chaired by the French then Commissioner Michel Barnier incorporated many of the proposals made by the four chocolate-producing governments, notably a diluted "solidarity clause," structured cooperation, and the European Defence Agency. Although the Convention may not have been in the driver's seat of ESDP, it seems that its taking place served as a catalyst for many ideas that had been floating around to be taken to a new level.[26] Parliamentarians took ownership of ESDP; experts testified at and commented on the Convention; the media paid attention, in part because the Convention was taking place during the worst period of the Iraq crisis; diplomats had to follow the work of the Convention and concentrate on each other's proposals.[27] French and German members were particularly active and tabled several joint proposals (De Schoutheete 2004). According to an individual who attended Defence Working Group meetings, as a result of this "constitutional effervescence," "the British representatives went perhaps a bit further in symbolic terms than they would have wanted to."[28]

Several ESDP-specific initiatives were debated, refined, and later adopted either by the Council or within the constitutional draft. First, the list of so-called Petersberg tasks, which forms the doctrinal basis of any EU crisis-management operation, was expanded to reflect what was perceived as the new strategic environment, including the threats posed by terrorism and failed states. Second, the possibility of structured cooperation in the area of defence was introduced under the guise of "greater flexibility." In doing away with the crippling problem of

[26] Interview with a member of the European Convention secretariat, Brussels, 2003.
[27] The rather impressive list of experts heard by the Defence Working Group reads like a who's who of the European security and defence field. It includes: Javier Solana (EU High Representative), Rainer Schuwirth (Head of EU Military Staff), Corrado Antonini (President of the European Defence Industries Group), Jean-Louis Gergorin (EADS), Laurent Giovacchini (French Delegation for Armaments), Peter Lundberg (Swedish Defence Equipment Agency), Anthony Parry (BAE Systems), Carlo Cabigiosu (former commander of KFOR), Alain Leroy (EU Special Envoy in FYROM), Gustav Hagglund (Chairman of EU Military Committee), Lord Robertson (NATO Secretary General), Alain Richard (former French Defence Minister), and Christopher Patten (EU Commissioner for External Relations).
[28] Interview with a member of the secretariat of the European Convention, Brussels, 2003.

unanimity, structured cooperation has served as the spirit if not the letter in establishing battle groups and decision-making procedures in the EDA. Third, a new mechanism was called for to finance the start-up costs of a military operation from a fund set up by the contributors; this became the Athena mechanism, which provides for common costs to be shared among EU members in the event of an EU operation. Fourth, a "solidarity clause" was introduced in the constitutional draft. Fifth, the Defence Working Group suggested that a Defence formation of the Council of Ministers be formally created. Last, the idea of a European Defence Agency received strong support.

Today, despite the failure of the Constitutional Treaty, the European Defence Agency and the EU's civilian–military planning cell are in place. Thanks to media coverage, the European Convention was a unique event that allowed a larger public to take an active interest in ESDP. While most of the delegates were appointed by the member states, the Convention provided a deliberative context that was probably less constraining than intergovernmental discussions. The actors who intervened were more or less the same who had been part of the ESDP community from the outset. But they could display more audacity in this environment; social skills were important. The expectation that they should table interesting, high-profile proposals was a local problem that governments and delegates needed to deal with. The prospect of finding a receptive audience was an incentive to *bricolage* institutional blueprints that would resonate with widely shared representations of European defence. In meetings that became more frequent, views were expressed with greater clarity, agreements were formalized, some ambiguities were put to rest: the picture of ESDP was fixed in the political landscape.

TRANSATLANTIC DISCORD AND THE EUROPEAN SECURITY STRATEGY

A final development that will no doubt shape ESDP is the European Security Strategy. Issued in 2003, the Security Strategy was born out of the EU's eagerness to find a response to Washington's new policy vis-à-vis terrorism and regime change. Ostensibly aimed at giving a coherent conceptual framework to ESDP, the Security Strategy sprang from, or was at least justified by, the terrorist attacks on New York City and the Pentagon and the American decision to topple the Iraqi regime.

Thinking on the conceptual underpinnings of ESDP had already begun under the Belgian presidency, in the second semester of 2001. Keenly interested in ESDP, the Belgian Defence Minister, André Flahaut, commissioned academics to explore the possibility of a White Paper on European defence (Biscop 2005). Discussions were held with diplomats and EU officials but the process remained informal. In October 2001, EU defence ministers tasked the EU Institute for Security Studies to work on a strategic concept for the EU—the term "White Paper" was seen as too ambitious or too constraining by several member states. The Institute brought the ESDP *intelligentsia* together: William Hopkinson (Royal Institute of International Affairs), François Heisbourg (Fondation pour la Recherche stratégique), Julian Lindley-French (EU Institute for Security Studies), Marc Otte (EU Council Secretariat), Nicole Gnesotto (EU Institute for Security Studies), Lothar Rühl (Stiftung Wissenschaft und Politik), and so on.[29] Their project was published in May 2004.

Although an official White Paper may never be issued, the Iraq War gave an impetus to move forward on conceptualizing the EU's strategic role. Public dismay over the lack of a common European position on Iraq, the Franco-German *rapprochement* as a reaction to it, and the ongoing European Convention created an incentive to try and define what would appear as a common EU position towards security challenges. In May 2003, at an informal meeting of the General Affairs Council, Javier Solana was officially tasked with drafting a report on the EU's security strategy. This, as Sven Biscop (2005) puts it, came as a "strategic surprise." Yet, Solana was able to table a draft at the Thessaloniki Summit only a month later, which suggests that conceptual work was already underway by the time Solana was officially requested to prepare a document. According to Christoph Meyer (2005: 538), the security strategy was proposed by COPS ambassadors, who "sold" their idea to their respective foreign ministers, who in turn tasked Solana to draft an EU strategy. The document was

---

[29] Together, these individuals account for a fair number of the writings on ESDP. See "European Defence: A Proposal for a White Paper," *Chaillot Paper.* Paris: European Union Institute for Security Studies, 2004.

prepared by officials close to Solana, with COPS input, and then approved by political directors.

Entitled, "A Secure Europe in a Better World," the final version of the European security strategy was adopted by EU leaders in December 2003. The security strategy purports to show that Europe shares American strategic concerns, and yet has a unique contribution to make on the world stage. The document lists five major threats: international terrorism, proliferation of weapons of mass destruction, regional conflicts, failing and failed states, and organized crime. These threats, the EU suggests, can be addressed with the tools of preventive engagement and effective multilateralism. In contrast to the US, the EU can provide humanitarian policing and soldiering, in conjunction with massive aid and development funds.

The initial wording and the structure of the security strategy were probably much influenced by the thinking of Robert Cooper who, after having played a role in Britain's 1998 volte-face when he was a senior Foreign Office diplomat, became Javier Solana's DG for Political and Military Affairs. While the document exhibits a fairly consensual tone, it shares with Cooper's book, *The Breaking of Nations*, a provocative commitment to "get real" and address hard security questions, without, however, going so far as to advocate the sort of liberal interventionism espoused by Cooper. The Security Strategy bears the imprint of the intellectual debate that took place around the Iraq War, illustrated by Robert Kagan's polemical contrast between a resolute America and a soft-bellied Europe, to which Cooper's book was a response. Solana's shop took this opportunity to enhance the EU's role in security and defence, in a manner reminiscent of what he had done with regards to terrorism after the Madrid bombings, with the creation of an EU counter-terrorism coordinator. The threat posed by "failed states," most of which would be in Africa, became yet another rationale for the development of ESDP.

The second impact of the Iraq War was to get the US army bogged down in Iraq, thus making it more appealing for the US to get out of the Balkans. British leaders often used the argument of freeing the US from its engagement in the Balkans to convince the Pentagon that ESDP could benefit them.[30] The argument became more compelling as the US focused its attention on Iraq. There were relatively few American troops left in the

---

[30] Interview with Lord Robertson, London, 2005.

Balkans but the US was still fully involved in running the NATO operation there. Given Washington's lingering reservations vis-à-vis ESDP, which the strong words of Nicholas Burns, the Undersecretary of State reminded us of not so long ago,[31] it is unlikely that the EU would have enjoyed such an easy ride in taking over the Bosnia mission had the US not had its attention elsewhere (Mérand 2007). As Posen (2006) argues, there is an element of "weak balance-of-power" here: those who believed in the strengthening of a European pole were helped by the US's relative weakening on the security front.

At the 2004 Istanbul Summit, NATO agreed to transfer most of its military operation in Bosnia to the EU. The EU took over on 2 December 2004, with Operation Althea, which is conducted by an EU Military Force (EUFOR) of about 7,000 troops. NATO continues to provide operational support to the EU Force under the Berlin Plus arrangements. The difference with SFOR is that US troops have left the force. In Washington, ESDP has become for its supporters a way for the Europeans to take on missions that are considered of low strategic relevance to the US. European officials, for their part, do not conceal that they see the Bosnia mission as a "test" of the EU's credibility. The region itself is relatively stable and may not require such a considerable military force. Moreover, the EU takeover has left the troops on the ground and the command structure virtually untouched. Arguably, EUFOR is more about the visibility and legitimacy of ESDP than foreign policy objectives per se.

The transatlantic discord was an external shock that had a profound and divisive impact on the European security community. European state actors could have responded in one of two ways. They could have drawn conclusions from European disunity and abandoned all hopes of an EU foreign and defence policy. But instead, ESDP was portrayed as an area where EU member states *could* find common ground while easing the burden on the US military. The European Security Strategy in particular did not follow logically from the St. Malo process. A number of scholars were advocating it, but it came as a "strategic surprise" to them when EU foreign ministers decided to move on. Its *delivery* in the year of the transatlantic discord was no coincidence. As to the *content* of the Security Strategy, it is better understood as a creative patchwork to deal with the

[31] Quoted in *EU Observer*, "EU's military capability is 'worrisome' ", 10 January 2005.

normative problem of European disunity, which the drafters sought to address with a US-inspired diagnosis and EU solutions, than as a rational design to espouse the new strategic environment.

CONCLUSION

By 2004, the European security and defence field described in Chapter 1 was in place. Its rapid development was a contingent and creative process, which involved the participation of an ever-expanding network of state actors around the core Franco-British axis. This new arena of interaction can rightly be described as a transgovernmental field, an expanding network of security and defence actors that cuts across national boundaries. Indeed, ESDP was designed behind closed doors, by a small community of more or less like-minded officials operating in an environment of relative public indifference, if not principled support. "ESDP experts" working for national foreign or defence ministries were likely to meet each other in Brussels more frequently than they met with their capital-based colleagues. Given a loose mandate to solve Europe's twin crisis of defence and diplomacy, these socially skilled state actors solicited ideas from outsiders, and seized on the opportunities offered by European and world politics to further a cooperative solution. Formally entrusted to defend the "national interest," they were in fact enacting transnational governance in their daily practice.

The success of this ambitious project can be attributed to the fact that, in contrast to previous "solutions," it does not threaten existing social representations or power structures. Symbolically, ESDP is a sort of *bricolage* whose ambiguous vocabulary conceals many opposing views (Lévi-Strauss 1961; Campbell 2004). Deeply held, social representations must be "translated" in an EU-level discourse that makes them palatable to other actors, especially politicians (Lascoumes 1996). There are, in ESDP, elements of transatlantic relationship and *Europe puissance*, of *Zivilmacht* and *Europe de la défense*, of English pragmatism and Gallic principles. It is built upon the intergovernmentalist logic dear to French and British diplomats, the federalist horizon of German diplomats, the *Europe puissance* motif of French diplomats, and the NATO military template known to defence policymakers. The international defence and the European foreign policy fields continue to live in ESDP. In fact, ESDP strengthens these fields: it bestows real capabilities to EU diplomats and legitimacy to Allied practices. But the result is a new way of organizing and talking about security in Europe, very much justified through the global discourse of "security governance" (Webber et al. 2004).

In terms of power structures, I have already mentioned the key role played by British and French officials. But it is interesting to note that, in the construction of ESDP, cleavages often ran less between countries such as France and the UK than between foreign policy and defence actors. Large sections of the French military establishment are as supportive of NATO as British policymakers are and German military officers may be as little attached to the concept of "superpower Europe" as British diplomats are (Bagayoko 2005*b*; Mérand 2006). That is, the interests of diplomats across the three countries are often closer to one another than they are to their own defence colleagues and vice versa. This can be attributed in large part to professional practices, which tend to resemble each other across national borders, but also to the internationalization of European armed forces and the Europeanization of foreign policy, which have made professional practices and social representations converge. While defence actors push for solutions to the problems of capabilities and interoperability, diplomats see themselves as involved in a larger game, which is to make the EU, and their countries within it, more influential in world affairs. When state actors have to work together, political alignments may not coincide with national boundaries but rather with organizational practices.

There is perhaps a third, more profound, reason for ESDP's success. I have noted that the political constraints on state actors were fairly loose, which allowed them to go about their work unencumbered by negative media campaigns or domestic veto threats, even in Britain and France, where public opinion is traditionally attached to national independence. Is defence no longer seen as a core attribute of state sovereignty? I explore this issue in the next, concluding chapter.

Conclusion

The European security and defence policy poses a twofold challenge to students of international politics. The first challenge specifically concerns the study of the EU. As I noted in the Introduction, European integration has been analysed since the 1950s through two dominant paradigms: neo-functionalism, which predicts ever closer union among European states as a result of their economic and legal integration, and intergovernmentalism, which expects that there will be political limits to this process of integration. From Ernst Haas and Stanley Hoffmann to Wayne Sandholtz and Andrew Moravcsik, the debate in EU studies has been largely about the extent of the national state's resilience in the face of economic integration. In Hoffmann's (1966) words, the question was whether the European state was "obstinate" or had been made "obsolete." Perhaps because of the early failure of the European Defence Community, and also because defence is construed as high politics *par excellence*, it was never seriously envisaged that defence policy could be Europeanized in the absence of a strong European *demos*.

The second challenge concerns the nature of the state and its place in the international system. Deep inside us, and at the heart of International Relations theory, lies the conviction that our primary allegiance goes to the national state and, further, that this political identity is more or less immutable. Dying for one's country remains the existential limit of one's political allegiance, and it is usually assumed to be the last attribute of national sovereignty—the blood tax. This conviction explains a fundamental, and often explicit, assumption in debates about European defence: namely that only when political identities converge will a common defence policy be possible. Much like diplomacy, International Relations theory remains deeply statocentric and, with a few exceptions, neglects the historical findings of the political sociology of Michael Mann,

Charles Tilly, and Pierre Bourdieu (Hobden and Hobson 2002). In the process of state formation, national identity did not necessarily come first.

In this concluding chapter, I take up these two challenges. I first argue that the rapid creation of a European security and defence field forces us to rethink the process of European integration. The inability of neo-functionalism and intergovernmentalism to theorize the development of European defence suggests that they may rest on a misunderstanding of the mechanisms of European integration (Ojanen 2006). I borrow from the new political–sociological approaches that are emerging in EU studies to make sense of the creation of a European security and defence field, and of European fields more generally.

Then I step back and reflect upon what the creation of a European security and defence field implies for the way we think about the state. I try to understand how it is possible that the state actors most closely associated with the formation of national states since the middle ages—namely statesmen, diplomats, and defence officials—are now working actively to supersede a key component of state sovereignty, thus enacting transnational governance from their positions in state capitals. This is where I argue that European defence is a symptom, but not a cause, of a broader transformation of the state in Europe, one in which the state is moving away from its core functions, the *"fonctions régaliennes"* that defined it for the past four centuries.

THE FIELDS OF EUROPEAN INTEGRATION

Over the past 10 years or so, a growing number of scholars have argued that theoretical debates about European integration were going nowhere. The attack originated from many different quarters. Anthropologists like Cris Shore (2000) in Britain and Marc Abélès (2000) in France came to the conclusion that Europe had reached such an advanced stage of integration that it made sense to shift one's attention from big causal arguments to fine-grained descriptions of the everyday practices of "building Europe." In the same vein, French and German political scientists sought to overcome the neofunctionalist/intergovernmentalist dichotomy by analysing how

European actors construct their own legitimacy in the process of implementing Community policies (Lequesne and Smith 1997; Héritier 1999). In Scandinavia and Britain, mostly, constructivists launched a frontal attack on mainstream International Relations theory. They made the case that EU scholars had neglected normative and ideational forces. Europe is a "normative power," pregnant with "symbols," and about which people have strong "ideas" (Christiansen, Jorgensen, and Wiener 1999; Risse 2004; Sjursen 2006). It cannot, they argued, be reduced to a concert of Europe where states exert their unbridled power. Neither is it appropriate to see the EU simply as a common market where governments bargain for economic advantage.

Political sociology was noticeably absent from these debates. By that, I mean that little attention was paid to the cross-national social forces, political cleavages, and power structures that are shaped and transformed by European integration (notable exceptions are found in Steenbergen and Marks 2004; and Bartolini 2005). As Virginie Guiraudon (2000), Niilo Kauppi (2003), Neil Fligstein (2008), and I, in this book, have argued, thinking in terms of *fields* is a fruitful way to uncover the social structures of European integration. To reiterate, a field is a structured arena of social interaction, wherein actors compete with each other to enhance their position and impose their "principles of vision and division." The development of the national state has been accompanied—was, in fact, *constituted*—by the institutionalization of a large number of national fields, for example, the literary field, the education field, or the political field. These national fields are well-entrenched and, as such, consequential for the actors who are involved in them and have internalized their *modus operandi*. Often centred upon the state, national fields are not about to disappear. But European integration can be conceptualized as the emergence and consolidation of a number of *transnational* fields, each with their own set of actors, power structures, and social representations. Using Bourdieusian vocabulary but relying on Karl Deutsch's insights, Fligstein (2008) discerns the development of transnational fields in areas as varied as football, the law, and high-tech industrial production. He defines Europeanization as the "process of building Europe-wide social arenas where people and organizations come to routinely interact." Some of these actors are players only in a given European field; most, however, are active in both a European and a national field.

European fields are erected upon existing national fields, which they can strengthen or undermine. For example, some national actors will use their involvement in the European field to bolster their position in the national field of power. This is allegedly the case with national judges, who have used the potentialities of Europe's quasi-constitutional order to strengthen their position vis-à-vis their own government (Weiler 1999; Vauchez 2007). Conversely, the creation of a European field can be detrimental to actors who held a privileged position in the national field but cannot quite make the European field work to their advantage. An illustration is provided by trade unions, which have been so far incapable of organizing themselves effectively on a European level, even though their influence on national governments is threatened by single market rules (Martin and Ross 1999; Wagner 2005).

In contrast to neofunctionalism, a political sociology based on fields would not necessarily predict that, as social interaction deepens, citizens and organizations will shift their loyalty to the new European centre. In fact, their involvement in European fields may be self-consciously instrumental in or even directly lead to a rejection of the European project itself. But, in contrast to intergovernmentalism, a field approach does make it possible for pan-European social integration to occur and generate policy outputs that escape the control of member states. There are a myriad social arenas where European integration proceeds unaided or unimpeded by the state; the Europeanization of football championships is a good example of this (King 2003). In other European fields, state actors are active, but they are not necessarily thinking in terms of promoting the national interest. Environmental policy and ESDP illustrate the way in which state actors promote Europeanization for reasons that have more to do with their professional interests than with domestic or international politics (McCormick 2001; Dezalay 2007).

Bourdieu's political sociology is more a conceptual tool box than a theory. It is flexible enough to accommodate a number of already existing theories of European integration. For example, fields provide a useful analytical angle on the "fusion hypothesis" propounded by Wolfgang Wessels (1997). For the German scholar, the externalities of socioeconomic interdependence have led European governments, in a rational pursuit of efficiency, to develop joint problem-solving instruments up to a point where one can speak of administrative fusion. State-based theories miss the extent to which the EU has become a complex politico-administrative system, with no real centre. Wessels' argument is compatible with the description of the EU by political scientists as a regime of multilevel governance or as a networked polity (Marks et al. 1996; Ansell 2000).

But characterizing the EU as an interdependent, multilevel system wherein decision-making is shared between many actors leaves many questions unanswered. Why did this network come about in Europe and not elsewhere? Who holds power in this system? According to which norms and rules are decisions made?

Although Bourdieu's conceptual framework does not give us an answer to all these questions, it does give us a lens through which actors, social representations, and considerations of power can be brought back into the multilevel picture. I think this book has provided evidence that ESDP has become a multilevel governance system or, as I called it, a transgovernmental field, wherein national and supranational, state and nonstate actors participate. While neofunctionalists would downplay the crucial role of national foreign and defence actors—they, not EU institutions, are the ones shaping ESDP—intergovernmentalists would have missed the impact of Brussels altogether. These positions can be reconciled by accepting that ESDP is a transgovernmental arena made up of actors from different fields: the international defence field and the European foreign policy field.

To these two important fields, which I describe at length in this book, Rathbun (2004) argues that we should add the national political field, where foreign policy issues are debated and mesh with partisan politics. Indeed, while mainstream politicians usually support European defence, left-of-centre parties tend to promote the civilian aspects of ESDP, which they think underpin the uniqueness of Europe's external role, while right-of-centre parties insist more on the importance of strengthening European military capabilities. Attitudes towards the European defence project are much more guarded on each extreme of the political spectrum, either because it is seen as an instrument of US domination (for the left) or because it threatens to undermine national sovereignty (for the right). In Britain, the Conservative Party is notoriously ambivalent about ESDP: while Tories have derided "*das EuroArmy*" in opposition, it is expected that they will display a certain form of pragmatism once they get into office, very much like they did with the EU more generally during the Major years.[1] Europeanized fields are not easy to deconstruct.

We need to go beyond the snapshot image of ESDP proposed by a multilevel governance approach. To analyse ESDP as a *field*, and thus pay attention to power structures and social representations, generates additional insights.

One such insight is that the ESDP field is deeply shaped by the interaction of foreign and defence policy actors. These actors are immersed in different contexts: the international defence field and the European foreign policy field, each with its set of actors, power structures, and social representations. Because they come from such different worlds, the interaction of diplomats and soldiers can often take the form of a cleavage. As I argued in Chapter 4, ESDP is for the military a means to improve their capabilities, while for diplomats, it is a means to enhance their political voice. Clashing frequently around the issue of whether ESDP should be capability- or policy-driven, the two groups try to bolster their position by shaping the European defence field in a way that they think will benefit them. ESDP thus becomes part of the strategies developed by foreign and defence policy actors to make sense of their social practices and increase their resources.

Thus, the ESDP field is a struggle about positions. But it is also a conflict of visions. These social representations are deeply embedded in national political fields. For the French, ESDP must lead to European *defence*; for the Germans, it serves to further European *integration*; for the British, it must remain a *policy*. Framing ESDP through the lens of their state traditions, policymakers also *project* onto ESDP their own representations of security: highly interventionist for the British and the French, who cannot imagine a defence policy without teeth, more integrationist for the Germans and small member states, who insist more on the federalist imagery of ESDP.

Consider the following illustration. When I asked Rudolf Scharping, the former defence minister of Germany, why he had taken such a great interest in ESDP, he snapped: "The deeper the integration, the smaller the room for national decision-making. I support the idea of European armed forces. National sovereignty *is* limited (emphasis mine)."[2] Such a bold statement of federal allegiance is, of course, unthinkable in a British

---

[1] Interviews, London, 2005.   [2] Interview with the author, Berlin, 2005.

or French context. But it does not mean a greater commitment to ESDP: just a different representation of what it is about. For Lord Robertson, who was Scharping's British counterpart in the late 1990s, the British volte-face at St. Malo was aimed at solving an "architectural problem," namely improving the effectiveness of European crisis management tools. But, he deplores, "there is an obsession with procedure rather than delivery."[3] When it comes to ESDP, the policy language of a British secretary is very different from the political language of a German minister.

Yet, a third vision is offered by a senior French diplomat who partic-ipated in the St. Malo discussions. In the French tradition of political theory, he says, the attributes of state sovereignty include first and foremost defence: "This is a tradition that goes back to Hughes Capet," the king who ruled France in the tenth century.[4] In the collective imagination of the French political class, a political authority *has* to have a defence arm, for it is part of the definition of sovereignty. This political representation does not imply support for European unification. But if sovereignty is transferred to the EU level, it is only normal that its attributes are also transferred. France probably remains the only country where one speaks lyrically of the "Europe of Defence," rather than the EU's defence policy, even though ESDP has little to do with the defence of a territory.

In other words, there is a symbolic dimension to the struggles that take place in the making and reproduction of a field. As Bourdieu reminded us, language is performative and, as such, entails a power dimension. Through symbols and rhetoric, actors try to shape a reality that will strengthen their position. This is what he calls "symbolic power." Being able to define what ESDP is and what it should do, that is, imposing one's social representa-tions onto the security and defence field, becomes a strategy of domina-tion, a way of controlling the incipient European field by mobilizing other actors behind one's project.

Thus understood, definitional struggles around ESDP, like the ones that often take place in Brussels think tanks or the comment pages of *The Financial Times*, appear less innocuous. A policy that focuses on increasing military capabilities will favour defence staffs and the armaments industry: not surprisingly, these two collective actors have been quick to support

---

[3] Interview, London, 2005.
[4] Interview, Ministère des Affaires étrangères, Paris, 2002.

the European Defence Agency. Defence firms like EADS or Thales also set shop in Brussels where they promote large-scale procurement projects like the Airbus A400M transport aircraft and the Galileo global positioning system. Conversely, a policy that focuses on civilian instruments, such as rule-of-law, police, and human security capabilities, will find a receptive audience among Commission officials, NGOs, and small countries with big development programmes, like Sweden and the Netherlands. Finally, there are some actors, notably foreign ministries and Council diplomats, who are keen that ESDP be used as often as possible and in riskier operations such as in the Congo, where they can serve to show that Europe's foreign policy and by extension their individual efforts are paying off.

THE CAUSES OF EUROPEANIZATION

Another question that this book has sought to address is how European fields come about. Methodologically, the key challenge is to theorize where, when, and how a new transnational field will emerge. The *sociogenesis* of a field, to use Bourdieu's term, requires a patient reconstruction of the *structural* conditions required for a field to emerge, and the specific *actions* that were taken in that regard. I have argued that the construction of a European defence field was made possible by, on the one hand, 50 years of military cooperation around NATO and, on the other, 50 years of European foreign policy cooperation around the EU. When, after the end of the Cold War, these two transgovernmental fields came into crisis, different solutions were proposed. The one that ultimately carried the day, ESDP, was elaborated and promoted by a relatively small group of state actors who managed to placate the sensibilities of politicians and foreign and defence ministries in France, the UK, and Germany, Europe's three military powers.

As Howorth (2003) has argued, the concept of "epistemic community" is a useful way of describing this group of actors. An epistemic community is a group of knowledge-based experts who minimally share a common set of factual and causal views, but often pursue the same organizational goals as well (Haas 1991; Cross 2006). In an epistemic community such as the one of European security officials, social representations about the role of the state, the nature of security problems, or organizational goals are likely to prevail over narrow definitions of interest, broad conceptions of culture, or domestic pressures. They can agree on institutional solutions because they share a certain number of practices and beliefs, but also because they have a strong professional interest in fulfilling the task they have been entrusted with.

It is often argued that the influence of this transgovernmental group of officials was strengthened, perhaps triggered, by two individuals: Prime Minister Tony Blair, who in Howorth's words "crossed the European defence Rubicon" after decades of British opposition, and Javier Solana, the EU High Representative, who used his considerable political capital and extensive networks acquired as a former NATO secretary general to move ESDP forward and, along the way, expand the scope of his EU Council Secretariat (Howorth 2000*a*; Buchet de Neuilly 2005). Without downplaying the role of these two charismatic, socially skilled leaders, I hope that this book has shown that their success owed a great deal to *structural* factors: namely the prior institutionalization of the international defence and European foreign policy fields, and the crises that these fields went through in the 1990s, both of which created the conditions and opportunities for ESDP to appear as a viable option.

Thus, the sociogenesis of a European field requires but goes beyond political entrepreneurship. A "networked polity" exists in Europe and not elsewhere because it is based on a myriad transnational fields that are densely populated and strongly institutionalized. New fields like European defence can emerge fairly easily from the interstices of existing fields, provided that the latter are themselves structured enough. Put differently, once a continent is crisscrossed with spheres of interaction, there are diminishing costs involved in setting up new fields. These new fields then take on a life of their own and, *ceteris paribus*, exert an ever increasing hold over their members. In other words, they become institutionalized as actors routinize their practices, power structures are reproduced, and social representations are internalized.

Though couched in Bourdieusian terms, this argument is congruent with much of political sociology, notably Michael Mann's (1986, 1993) theory of social change, which stresses not only the institutionalization of power networks but also the "interstitial emergence" of new forms of power relations between the pores of pre-existing power networks.

Overlapping networks, says Mann, are often created at the intersection of other, more established, forms of social interaction. For example, influential economic groups emerged interstitially from the political scope of empires, which provided secure trading routes and a common language for conducting business. In the same way, one could say that ESDP relies on the culture of cooperation developed in the international defence field and the intense political activity associated to the European foreign policy field.

Indeed, the causes of European integration are often to be found in long-term factors. The production and reproduction of fields will often have unanticipated consequences. They can "stick" out of habit or because actors have invested so much energy in them, even when the purpose of the field is no longer seen as self-evident. They can also yield new institutional forms that are simply "layered" onto old ones. This argument will be known to readers as historical institutionalism, which has been applied with some success to understand the creeping competences of EU institutions (Pierson 1996). The story told in this book is slightly different, though, because it also stresses the contingency and creativity involved in structuring new transnational fields. Institutional development is not necessarily cumulative. While it depends a great deal on prior institutional forms like the international defence field, the rise of ESDP also owes to trial-and-error or, as Mann calls it, "cock-up-foul-up theory."

Options considered in the past may disappear altogether: that was the fate of the European security and defence identity, developed between 1994 and 1996 to give the Europeans a greater say in the Atlantic Alliance; despite a long list of official communiqués and declarations, no one is thinking of resurrecting ESDI. It left its imprint on the EU's military chain of command through the role of DSACEUR but gone is the idea that, politically, Europeans would be best organized *inside* NATO.[5] Other options may be tried and abandoned: long seen as the future defence arm of the EU, the WEU was thought beyond repair after 1999 and discarded. It is no longer conceivable either that the OSCE, the only pan-European

[5] Even though ESDI and ESDP share common operational features, ESDP differs from its precursor in several ways: (1) the EU is the sole political decision-maker; (2) institutionally, the WEU is out of the picture; (3) although NATO assets may be borrowed by the EU, such as is the case in Bosnia, the emphasis is now on the development of *autonomous* planning and addressing capability gaps with a view to conducting *autonomous* operations. In other words, while ESDI was a capability-based transatlantic project, ESDP is arguably a politically driven EU project (Brenner 2002: 7; Salmon and Shepherd 2003: 170).

security organization, will play a predominant role in the continent's security policy. Finally, certain possibilities arise outside the path of institutional development. An "ESDP for Africa" did not proceed straight from the institutional development of ESDP but from external factors that were filtered and utilized by ESDP actors who, incidentally, could count on an already Europeanized field for development and humanitarian aid. In this sense, the *form* taken by ESDP was contingent on the actions of specific groups of individuals, but the fact of European security and defence *cooperation* was not: to carry the day, any credible option had to satisfy both soldiers and diplomats, most probably through some form of *rapprochement* between the international defence and European foreign policy fields.

To return to a discussion begun in the Introduction, an important element in European military integration is that it is taking place in the context of strong economic, but weaker political and ideological, integration. To a large extent, proponents of ESDP can count on the strong support of defence firms and the Commission, both of which are keen to strengthen the European industrial base. The restructuring of Europe's corporate sector since the mid-1980s, launched by the Single Market liberalization programme, is certainly one reason why hurdles to multinational armaments cooperation have all but disappeared. Since the mid-1990s, the defence industry has been Europeanizing fast, with the result that the defence industry is now a key ally for ESDP proponents, whereas in the past it was often painted as an opponent (Moravcsik 1993).

Europeanists can also, to some extent, rely on the dense institutional fabric of political cooperation in Europe. But while there is a lot of cooperation going on, political integration is hampered by the rigid decision-making procedures of the EU's foreign policy machine. The limits of a consensus-based decision-making system are well known. In Chapter 1, we saw how the variety of social representations held by foreign and defence policy actors can often act as a break on the development of ESDP. These problems are amplified by the weakness of ideological integration in Europe. The presence of several political and military cultures among the 27 member states testifies to the resilience of symbolic perceptions produced by the national state (Cornish and Edwards 2001; Rynning 2003; Meyer 2006). Taking place at the elite level, European military integration is unlikely to bring ordinary citizens into its fold. It will not generate ideological integration in the same way that, through conscription, national armed forces promoted national identities in the nineteenth century. All of this suggests that European military integration is unfolding in a context that is very different from the process of political and ideological integration that accompanied the creation of national armies. European defence is not, like the creation of national armies was, a product of the need to wage war; it is, on the contrary, an offshoot of the *absence* of war.

Mann's notion of "interstitial emergence" should caution us against teleological explanations of the development of ESDP. There has been a tendency among ESDP scholars to take political actors' self-justifications at face value. As I remarked in Chapter 5, the purpose of ESDP was altered many times, and continues to differ depending on who the social scientist speaks to. Quite naturally, informers working in the EU Council or in a defence ministry will often present the "current" priority of ESDP as the reason why it was launched. Talking to British diplomats in 1999 may convince their interlocutor that London agreed to ESDP because "they realized they had failed to stop the massacre in Kosovo." Interviewing the same officials today may lead us to think that the real cause of ESDP was the need for Europe to assume its proper role in the transatlantic relationship, notably by strengthening its military capabilities. The list of proximate "causes" is endless. For the social scientist, accepting these claims uncritically carries the risk of mistaking the real *modus operandi* (the practice of building ESDP) for what Bourdieu calls the *opus operatum* (the end result).

STATE TRANSFORMATION AND EUROPEAN DEFENCE

One way of looking at the construction of European defence is to argue that it is part and parcel of the internationalization of the state (Wendt 1994). For social theorists like Chris Rumford (2002: 70), the EU is a "new kind of state" that encapsulates the trends and tensions of globalization, a process which means the demise of nationally bounded societies. Somewhat similarly, Martin Shaw (2000) argues that we are witnessing the emergence of a global state: power structures are so enmeshed with each other, at least in the West, that it makes little sense for him to speak of a national "power container" anymore. The EU, the argument goes, is just a part of this phenomenon. David Held (1999: 144), for his part, provides a more sober assessment, noting that there is a "multilayered and multilateral system of governance for Atlantic defence and security matters complementing domestic structures and processes." Held still speaks of "military globalization," but it is not clear whether, for him, military globalization has really been achieved or, as is more likely, whether rather it constitutes the necessary outcome of the "cosmopolitan democracy" he is calling for. In any event, the "globalization/internationalization of the state" thesis views European integration as an instance of globalization—not, as Perry Anderson would have it, a process *sui generis*.[6]

I take a slightly different view here. The globalization/internationalization of the state thesis gives the impression that no one really controls this "global concentration of power." It is as if states had lost control in a diffuse integration of military institutions. We know that this is not true: by and large, state actors remain in charge, even in the EU. However, the idea that the monopoly of legitimate coercion would have moved to the EU level, thus making it a superstate, does not stand up to scrutiny either. A fully fledged European Army may be created sooner than most people expect, but it will not be controlled by a supranational executive like the European Commission. By ricochet, Washington is more likely to play a meaningful role than the EU's executive, much as it did since the 1950s. Mark Webber et al. (2004) and his colleagues describe a more plausible scenario when they speak of a European security *governance* system, one in which actors are more numerous, practices more homogenous across states, but state actors and national practices remain dominant.

Still, I think these different characterizations miss the most important point. Military integration is certainly not ushering in the creation of a European superstate, but it does amount to a partial surrender on the part of state actors of their monopoly over legitimate violence. Clearly, defence policy is being denationalized in Europe. On the one hand, it has become almost impossible for national authorities to launch procurement programmes or to deploy military contingents without taking European institutions and other governments into account. In the two communiqués

---

[6] Perry Anderson. "Under the Sign of the Interim," *London Review of Books*. 4 January 1996.

that announced the building of a second aircraft carrier on a common Franco-British platform, Jacques Chirac, the French President, character-istically explained his decision with three reasons: protecting the security of French citizens; promoting the Europe of defence; and enhancing coop-eration with the UK.[7] More recently, European contributions to the UN Interim Force II in Lebanon were the object of intense discussions between EU capitals, notably Paris and Rome. Increasingly, "Europe" is factored in national defence policymaking. As I mentioned earlier in the book, there is today not a single "national" military operation conducted by an EU state.

On the other hand, national decision-making processes are deeply affected by EU developments. In Paris as in Berlin, the reform of the armed forces has been explicitly justified in terms of strengthening European defence (King 2005). The abolition of conscription was undertaken in France and is advocated in Germany as a means to make the national armed forces compatible with the force structure of an EU rapid reaction force (Sarotte 2001; Irondelle 2003*b*). In the German defence ministry, reducing the reliance on conscripts, creating a multinational joint plan-ning cell, and bolstering rapid reaction units were regularly presented to the author as part of a package aimed at strengthening ESDP. Although some of these claims may be self-serving in the sense that reforms would have been made even without ESDP in place, ESDP has certainly led to a permanent state of benchmarking among European defence ministries.

These two trends have led Bastien Irondelle (2003*a*) to argue that we are witnessing "Europeanization without the European Union." The puzzle is that this denationalization of defence policy is being carried out by the historical carriers of state sovereignty: statesmen, diplomats, and military officers. How are we to account for this? Are state actors bringing about their own demise?

The answer provided in this book is that the deep and broad interpen-etration of European states has created strong incentives for state actors to coordinate their foreign and defence policies at an EU level. "Inter-nationalization" and more specifically "Europeanization" have constituted a single strategy on the part of state actors to salvage their positions by giving them access to more resources and enhancing their legitimacy. By

---

[7] Communiqué de la présidence relatif au projet de Loi de programmation militaire, 11 Septembre 2002; Communiqué de la présidence relatif au type de propulsion du deuxième porte-avions français, 13 février 2004.

downplaying patriotism and stressing the "politics of scale," this strategy gave meaning to professional practices that would have otherwise be seen as antiquated in late twentieth century Europe. This is what the international defence field (through NATO) and the European foreign policy field (through the EU) provided diplomats and soldiers with since the early 1950s.

The end of the Cold War and the travails of European politics threatened this internationalization/Europeanization strategy. After many attempts, ESDP emerged against the backdrop of 50 years of intense military and foreign policy cooperation among Europeans, in the EU but also in NATO. In an important way, however, European defence goes far beyond the common foreign policy and the military alliance. The fact that it could be put in place without any substantial opposition demonstrates the possibility of a dramatic shift in the very nature of the state. More specifically, European military integration was made possible—and is likely to go further—*because defence has lost its centrality in people's understanding of the state.* NATO may have been the harbinger of this transformation, but its "collective identity" rested on a defence pact against a known enemy. In stark contrast, ESDP is explicitly aimed at no one: for its planners as for the general public, military integration is an end in and of itself.

For a European born after the creation of the EU, it is hard to imagine what the state used to represent for its citizens. As Eugen Weber (1974) documented in his history of late nineteenth century France, social representations of the state were embodied in the universal (male) experience of military conscription. It is not surprising, then, that "legitimate coercion" constituted the essence of Max Weber's definition of the state around the turn of the century. Until the 1960s, most French, German, or British males would have fought (i.e. as *soldiers*) in at least one military conflict in their lives. War and the national state were tightly interwoven as the industrialization of war and the mass army format turned out a steady flow of citizens caged in national structures of mobilization.

Throughout the nineteenth and early twentieth century, defence constituted the primary task and budgetary line of national states. Usually around 3–5% during these two centuries, the military burden (ratio of defence spending to GDP) of countries like France or Britain could rise to 50% in wartime—and wartime occurred often. Meanwhile, social spending in these two countries (welfare, pensions, health, housing) was consistently under 1.5% of GDP until the mid-1920s (Lindert 2004). Even then, as Eloranta (2004) points out, these figures conceal the real importance of defence as a proportion of *public expenditures* in that era: "In the French case, the defence share [i.e. the ratio of defence spending to public expenditures] stayed roughly the same, a little over 30 percent, throughout the nineteenth and early twentieth centuries ... In the UK case, the defence share mean declined two percent to 36.7 percent in 1870–1913, compared to early nineteenth century." European states spent anywhere from 3 to 50 times more on defence than they did on social policy.

The situation is now completely reversed. Today, the state is characterized by its social functions. The figures are striking. As a percentage of GDP, defence expenditure in EU states decreased by ~70% over the past three decades and are now around 2%. By comparison, social expenditure stands today at around 25–30% of GDP. West European countries spend almost 10 times less on defence than they do on social policies. The number of citizens in uniform has also been cut by almost 50% over the same period, and conscription, which meant that every male citizen had had some experience with in the military, sometimes for as long as 3 to 7 years, has been abolished or drastically reduced in most of Western Europe. What Theda Skocpol (1992) and Stefano Bartolini (2005) describe as the transition from the warfare to the welfare state is also evident in political demands, where military issues play an ever diminishing role. Table C.1 depicts political demands vis-à-vis government spending in Great Britain and Germany. *Mutatis mutandis*, it shows that large majorities of British and German citizens want public spending increases for the environment, health, old age pensions, and education; conversely, there is also a substantial majority in Germany and a plurality in Britain who want defence budgets to be *decreased*. For most Europeans, the state no longer means defence policy.

While many scholars have pointed to instances of (re)securitization in the discourse and practices of European states, especially since September 11, I would therefore argue, following Martin Van Creveld (1999), that the late twentieth century's most profound transformation in Europe was *demilitarization*. This forces us to rethink Weber's definition of the state by moving away from its military origins and towards its symbolic functions, which are nowadays expressed through social polices. As Bourdieu argued, the monopoly over legitimate *physical* violence may no

Table C.1. Public opinion on perceived necessary changes in government spending, various policy sectors (in %)[i]

	1985–6		1996	
	Increase	Decrease	Increase	Decrease
Germany				
Environment	82.6	1.5	58.6	5.4
Health	52.3	7.2	53.8	6.8
Education	40.1	7	51.2	6.8
Military and defence	6.2	63.2	8.2	66.2
Old age pensions	46.4	3.9	44.4	4.9
Great Britain				
Environment	37	5.5	44.6	5.7
Health	88	0.8	91.5	0.4
Education	74.8	2	84.5	0.9
Military and defence	17.8	37.1	18.6	33.4
Old age pensions	75.1	1.2	80	0.8

[i] The balance consists of individuals who say that government spending in this policy sector should remain the same.

Source: ICPSR *Role of Government I–III* (nos. 8909 and 2808).

longer be as important as its monopoly over legitimate *symbolic* violence. The strictly coercive dimension of state power, encapsulated by Tilly's description of state-making as "organized crime," has given way to more subtle practices of legitimation, surveillance, and ways of responding to social demands. The military becomes a *service*, which can be offered, shared, and reconfigured, and not a key attribute of the state.

The national state, in turn, has lost its hold over military allegiance, or the formation of exclusive identity attachments through the military institution. Today, European armed forces are far more likely to be deployed in a multinational context than in a national one. The multinational context may be provided by the UN, NATO, the EU, or an ad hoc coalition. Whether they like it or not, soldiers wear an international organization badge next to their national flag (Moskos, Allen, and Segal 2000). This has led some scholars to speak of a "cosmopolitan military" (Elliott and Cheeseman 2004; Terriff 2004). But this description does not quite fit with another emerging trend, which is the privatization of military force. As Peter Singer (2002) describes in *Corporate Warriors*, an increasing number of professional soldiers, often retired from active duty, fight and risk their lives for private firms (cf. also Avant 2005). Martin Van Creveld (1999: 407) even suggests that "the conduct of violence may revert to what it was as late as the first half of the seventeenth century: namely a capitalist enterprise little different from, and intimately linked with, so many others." Again, what this suggests is that the 400-year-old link between the military profession and the national state is not as strong as it used to be.

In a survey conducted in 1992, it was found that most European soldiers do not join the forces for patriotic reasons, but for professional reasons (Mérand 2003). With historical hindsight, this should not be too surprising. Before it became a core element of the sovereign state, the military institution had known many forms. The *Condottiere* fought for money and honour. Aristocratic armies, like those found in the late middle ages or later in the Austro-Hungarian Empire, were loyal to a ruler, not to a state. They formed a caste whose national attachment was tenuous at best (Deak 1990). As Otto Hintze wrote (1975: 200), they were "a foreign body in the state." It is only in the nineteenth and early twentieth century that mass armies, often made up of conscripts whose national allegiance had been forced upon them by years of national education, national literature, and national wars, developed a strong connection to nationalism (Posen 1993). *Pro patria mori* is an old idea, but only in the context of the national state, crystallized as a militarist enterprise, did it pervade society (Kantorowicz 1951).

Allegiance is a flexible and malleable category. Identification with the national state was and certainly continues to be strong. But in Europe, the reasons for this national allegiance are increasingly found in the symbolic (e.g. *laïcité* in France; parliamentarism in Britain; football in Britain or Germany) or social (e.g. the welfare state in Nordic countries; pensions in France or Italy) functions of the state. These reasons are varied and prone to change. As Rogers Brubaker argues (1996: 19), nationness is "something that suddenly crystallizes, a contingent, conjuncturally fluctuating, and precarious frame of vision and basis for collective action." While the military institution remains quite popular, the available data shows that, in France and in Germany, willingness to die for one's country (admittedly a poor and self-reported measure of military patriotism) is not widespread. Depicted on Table C.2, the figures are especially telling

Table C.2. Willingness to fight for your country: France and Germany (1999)

Base = 3651 weight (with split ups)	Total		France (1999)		West Germany (1999)		East Germany (1999)	
	n	(%)	*N*	(%)	*n*	(%)	*n*	(%)
No	1387	38.0	568	35.2	417	40.2	401	40.2
Yes	1437	39.4	778	48.2	381	36.7	278	27.8
Do not know	626	17.1	193	12.0	183	17.6	250	25.0
No answer	201	5.5	75	4.6	56	5.4	69	7.0
Total	3651	100	1615	100	1037	100	999	100

Source: World Values Survey, ASEP/JDS Databank.

given the abolition of conscription in most European countries, which has severed the link between the "citizen-in-arms" and the national state. Unfortunately, there is no data on "willingness to die for Europe." But the popularity of European defence, which it is worth repeating is for greater than that of the EU itself, suggests that the role of the armed forces is no longer so tightly linked to the exercising of national sovereignty. While this does not mean that one allegiance is likely to supersede the other, it does create ample room for military integration.

POLITICAL SOCIOLOGY AND INTERNATIONAL RELATIONS

In the light of this *public* indifference to "national" defence, the deeply held notion among IR scholars that defence policy is the key attribute of state sovereignty—and therefore cannot be pooled or delegated—becomes problematic. Indeed, most of the literature on military integration, which is more often than not a literature on military *alliances*, assumes that states will pool their resources only if their vital interests are threatened by a third party—the example of choice, of course, being NATO (Walt 1987). Remove such a threat, and military integration becomes a theoretical impossibility.[8] As Kenneth Waltz (1979: 107) writes, "states do

---

[8] For an attempt to nuance this argument by allowing for the possibility that states may discover incentives to create a military alliance, see Wallander, Haftendorn, and Keohane (1999).

not willingly place themselves in situations of increased dependence. In a self-help system, considerations of security subordinate economic gain to political interest."

The following phrase by Jolyon Howorth (2000*b*: 82), which I quoted in the Introduction, is typical of the assumptions we (the author included) have a tendency to make about the national state–armed forces nexus. Howorth writes,

Ever since the 1950s, when Jean Monnet, buoyed by the success of the Coal and Steel Community, decided to try to apply the same supranational method to the European Defence Community, it has been clear to most analysts that, while one can decide steel quotas by committee, one cannot send young men to die in a foreign field by qualified majority voting.

True enough, as things currently stand. But unless one reifies the national state, one wonders why that should be so "clear" to analysts, for sending young men to die in a foreign field by QMV or by decree is precisely what national states, empires, warlords, and private firms have been doing for many centuries. Democratic legitimacy rarely had anything to do with it.

Now, it could very well be that, today, sovereignty is anchored so deeply to the people's identity through democracy and political participation that political leaders really need to cater to their statocentric constituency. A relatively benign security environment post-1989 would have merely put these concerns under a blanket. In other words, statocentrism may be a social construct, but it is a deeply institutionalized one and so it makes sense to treat it as a fact. Notwithstanding the problem that this would give a lot of credit to democratic institutions in shaping foreign policy, it is sufficient to reiterate that public opinion is in fact extremely supportive of Europeanization efforts in the area of defence policy, at least in this benign environment. Thus, if state sovereignty remains paramount in official and academic discourse, this has more to do with self-perceptions on the part of state actors and our own lack of critical distance vis-à-vis them.

Once again, Bourdieu makes two suggestions that can help us break free from the "common sense" (what he calls *doxa*) of International Relations theory. First, Bourdieu cautions us that the state is not an actor or an

---

For a critique of the interest-based argument that chooses to stress a shared identity, see Risse-Kappen (1995). In both cases, however, states remain the sole actors in this process: they are the ones that have "interests" and "identities."

essence, but a *structure*. In other words, the state is a deeply fractious field of social relations wherein different actors vie to impose their "principles of vision and division." To speak on behalf of the state is to stake a claim to the state's legitimacy and resources in order to position oneself in the field of power. Bourdieu's approach opens up the black box of the state. Different state actors may pursue different aims. Diplomats and military officers are not necessarily defending "the" national interest. This, as we have seen, goes some way towards explaining ESDP, which emerged in spite of what were seen as conflicting "state interests." If one begins with the centrality and immutability of the state as a postulate, it is implausible that something like the development of ESDP can be understood.

Second, and this has more profound epistemological consequences, Bourdieu challenges the view that the categories produced by the state (such as "state interest," "national identity," or "democratic legitimacy") can be borrowed uncritically by the social scientist, at least without losing purchase on social practices. "To endeavour to think the state," Bourdieu writes (1994: 99), "is to take the risk of taking over (or being taken over by) a thought of the state, i.e., of applying to the state categories of thought produced and guaranteed by the state and hence to misrecognize its most profound truth." It is difficult to break with state-based principles of vision and division. As citizens and social scientists, we have naturalized the categories used by state actors, which we borrow and legitimize. The most damaging one, so central to the modern project, is to think of the state as a primordial actor and of the national state as the impassable horizon of our lives. This is what Jan-Aart Scholte (2000) and Ulrich Beck and Edgar Grande (2007) have recently called our "methodological nationalism."

Political sociology can provide conceptual ammunition to the growing community of International Relations scholars who are questioning the naturalness of the state in their analyses. In particular, I believe that a coherent research programme can come out of a richer dialogue between political sociology and some versions of constructivism. When tapping into sociology's resources, constructivists have had a tendency to limit themselves to Anthony Giddens and his theory of "structuration," which has enabled them to conceptualize how state identities are contingent and mutually constitutive. Giddens' work on the historical origins of the state, whose insights are largely congruent with Bourdieu's, Mann's, and Tilly's, have been left largely untouched. The result has been a theoretical commitment to put the identity of the state in context, but not the state itself. By identifying the struggles and power networks that shape the state from below, from the inside, and from above, political sociology can be called upon to establish a link between constructivism and nonessentialist International Relations approaches, such as Allison's (1971) bureaucratic politics model.

Also, constructivists can find sympathetic if critical interlocutors among political sociologists in their concern for ideas and norms. By and large, political sociology adheres to Max Weber's dictum that there are neither ideas nor interests, but ideational and material interests. Dichotomies are not productive. For Mann, ideas, riches, force, and authority can all be sources of power and social action. For Bourdieu, ideas and interests are two facets of the same practical attitude, which is that actors have structure-induced dispositions towards the world (*habitus*) and are genuinely interested in paying the social game over which they have little control (*illusio*). What distinguishes these approaches from a certain strand of constructivism is that power and conflict over resources, whether symbolic or material, are at the heart of the analysis. Power struggles are always a way of interpreting and engaging with the symbolic world, but they do matter concretely. For political sociology, ideas matter because they are *embodied* in concrete social practices, but it is not "ideas all the way down" (Wendt 1999, Williams 2006).

WHITHER EUROPEAN DEFENCE?

Assuming that European military integration goes forward, and it is reasonable to think that it will, to a greater or smaller extent, in an institutional framework that mixes supranational, intergovernmental, and transgovernmental elements, an important question is whether European defence is *desirable*. This concern is voiced by a number of citizens, many of whom are not nationalists. Would Europe not betray the project of perpetual peace that lied at its foundation if it took a military dimension? Should Europe not "dissolve into its own effects" and become a model of international law and peaceful resolution of conflicts (Balibar 2003)? Does the European identity not stem from its unique civilian role? Does it make sense to speak of a "defence" policy for a project that specifically aims at doing away with borders?

Two polar opposites in this debate were François Duchêne (1972), who believed that Europe's uniqueness rested with its civilian status, and Hedley Bull (1982), for whom military power was crucial to determine whether the EU would move towards a quasi-state status. The issue is far from being settled. But, in this important philosophical debate, something should not be forgotten. In its current and most likely form, European defence is not meant to herald the emergence of a superpower; it is sold to European citizens as a way to ensure that, when it comes to solving humanitarian and political crises such as Bosnia, the Congo, or Palestine, Europe can put its money where its mouth is. Some form of military backup is the only way for Europe to defend its unique perspective on conflict resolution. In these troubled times of ours, the world desperately needs a different voice. As Stanley Hoffmann, the Austrian-born, French-raised American, wrote in the columns of *Le Monde* on 6–7 June 1999: "Europe must not remain an economic giant and a diplomatic and military dwarf; in the long run, its weakness in the latter domains will sap its forces in others."

But perhaps European defence has more to do with the continent's own future than with its international influence. Very shortly after the end of the Cold War, as initial fears of chaos dissipated, it appeared that the core of Europe would not revert to its turbulent, military conflict-prone past. This in itself is one of the most comforting phenomena of the last century. Theories abound as to why Europe did not break apart. Of course, a number of scholars predicted that the current stability was only transitory. With the passing of time, old rivalries would resurface, new power conflicts would erupt. Some, rediscovering the virtues of liberal theory, reiterated the pacifying influence of the market, which had dominated Western Europe since World War II and had swept through the rest of the continent in the aftermath of 1989. Others pointed to the existence of a common civilization, in the most culturalist accounts; a security community, in more institutional ones; in any event, a sense of we-feeling among West European and North Atlantic peoples that made military competition almost unthinkable. The cruel memory of past bloodsheds had taught them that wars engendered more suffering than benefits. Still others argued that, notwithstanding the official end of the bipolar system, the autonomy of European states remained constrained by the superpower squeeze: the shadow of Russia and the US ensures that the region remains a stable one. Finally, it is possible that Europe and the transatlantic community projected peace onto the continent through the prospect of EU and NATO enlargement, which promised many benefits that will take some time to assess.

A combination of these factors probably led to the peace and security Europe (with the notable exception of the Balkans) enjoyed in the post-Cold War era. However, one cannot help but worry about how long this blissful state will last. While it may seem remote to the citizens and academics of prosperous countries, the possibility that war could break out one day between two or more European states remains present. None of the factors above-mentioned is, in and of itself, sufficient to prevent conflicts from re-emerging; none is eternal either. Suffice it that international order be upset by a transformation of America's attitude towards European security, or that economic integration under the auspices of the single market grinds to a halt, and *pax europea* could be endangered. In this sense, neorealists are right: the sudden hardening of the security environment would be a real test for the analysis presented in this book. In the long run, the only safe way to prevent the re-emergence of interstate military conflict in Europe as well as the security of the continent is to further integrate the military instruments of European states: in the words uttered by Robert Schuman on 9 May 1950, "to make war materially impossible." If successful, the greatest contribution of the European security and defence policy might be to make defence policy itself irrelevant.

References

Abélès, Marc (2000). *La vie quotidienne au Parlement Européen*. Paris: Hachette.

Adler, Emanuel (1998). "Seeds of Peaceful Change: The OSCE's Security Community-Building Model," in *Security Communities*, edited by E. Adler and M. Barnett. Cambridge: Cambridge University Press.

—— and M. Barnett (eds.) (1998). *Security Communities*. Cambridge: Cambridge University Press.

Allison, Graham (1971). *Essence of Decision: Explaining the Cuban Missile Crisis*. Boston: Little, Brown.

Anderson, Benedict (1983). *Imagined Communities: Reflections on the Origins and Spread of Nationalism*. London: Verso.

Anderson, Stephanie and T. R. Seitz (2006). "European Security and Defense Policy Demystified," *Armed Forces & Society*. 33(1): 24–42.

Andersson, Jan Joel (2006). *Armed and Ready? The EU Battlegroup Concept and the Nordic Battlegroup*. Stockholm: Swedish Institute for European Policy Studies.

Andréani, Gilles, C. Bertram, and C. Grant (2001). *Europe's Military Revolution*. London: Centre for European Reform.

Ansell, Christopher (2000). "The Networked Polity: Regional Development in Western Europe," *Governance*. 12(3): 303–33.

Aron, Raymond and D. Lerner (1956). *L'échec de la CED. Essais d'analyse sociologique*. Paris: A. Colin.

Art, Robert J. (2004). "Europe Hedges Its Security Bets," in *Balance of Power: Theory and Practice in the 21st Century*, edited by T. V. Paul, J. Wirtz, and M. Fortmann. Stanford: Stanford University Press.

Asmus, Ronald D., R. L. Kugler, and F. S. Larrabee (1993). "Building a New NATO," *Foreign Affairs*. 72(4): 28–40.

Avant, Deborah (2005). *The Market for Force: The Consequences of Privatizing Security*. Cambridge: Cambridge University Press.

Aybet, Gülnur (2001). *The Dynamics of European Security Cooperation*. Houndmills: Palgrave.

Bagayoko, Niagalé (2005a). "Les politiques européennes de prévention et de gestion des conflits en Afrique subsaharienne," *Les champs de mars*. 16: 93–114.

—— (2005b). "L'européanisation des militaires français: Socialisation institutionnelle et culture stratégique," *Revue française de science politique*. 56(1): 49–77.

Balibar, Etienne (2003). *L'Europe, quelle puissance?* Paris: La Découverte.

Bartolini, Stefano (2005). *Restructuring Europe: Centre Formation, System Building and Political Structuring between the Nation-State and the European Union.* Oxford: Oxford University Press.

Baumann, Rainer (2001). "German Security Policy within NATO," in *German Foreign Policy Since Unification: Theories and Case Studies*, edited by V. Rittberger. Manchester: Manchester University Press.

Beck, Ulrich and E. Grande (2007). *Cosmopolitan Europe.* Cambridge: Polity.

Biscop, Sven (2005). *The European Security Strategy: A Global Agenda for Positive Power.* London: Ashgate.

Bloch-Laine, Amaya (1999). "Franco-German Cooperation in Foreign Affairs, Security and Defence: A Case Study," in *The Franco-German Relationship in the European Union*, edited by D. Webber. London: Routledge.

Bodenheimer, Susanne (1967). *Political Union: A Microcosm of European Politics, 1960–1966.* Leyden: Sijthoff.

Boëne, Bernard (2003). "The Military as a Tribe Among Tribes: Postmodern Armed Forces and Civil-Military Relations," in *Handbook of the Sociology of the Military*, edited by G. Caforio. New York: Kluwer.

Bourdieu, Pierre (1980). *Le sens pratique.* Paris: Minuit.

—— (1989). *La noblesse d'état: Grandes écoles et esprit de corps.* Paris: Minuit.

—— (1994). "Esprits d'état: Genèse et structure du champ bureaucratique," in *Raisons pratiques: Sur la théorie de l'action*, edited by P. Bourdieu. Paris: Le Seuil.

—— (1997). *Méditations pascaliennes.* Paris: Le Seuil.

—— (2000). *Les structures sociales de l'économie.* Paris: Le Seuil.

—— (2001). *Langage et pouvoir symbolique.* Paris: Fayard.

—— and L. Wacquant (1992). *An Invitation to Reflexive Sociology.* Chicago: University of Chicago Press.

Brenner, Michael (2002). *Europe's New Security Vocation.* Washington: National Defense University.

Britz, Malena and A. Eriksson (2005). "The European Security and Defence Policy: A Fourth System of European Foreign Policy?" *Politique européenne.* 17: 35–62.

Brubaker, Rogers (1996). *Nationalism Reframed: Nationhood and the National Question in the New Europe.* Cambridge: Cambridge University Press.

Buchet de Neuilly, Yves (2005). *L'Europe de la politique étrangère.* Paris: Economica.

Budden, Philip (2002). "Observations on the Single European Act and the 'Relaunch of Europe': A Less Intergovernmental Reading of the 1985 Intergovernmental Conference," *Journal of European Public Policy.* 9(1): 76–97.

Bull, Hedley (1982). "Civilian Power Europe: A Contradiction in Terms?" *Journal of Common Market Studies.* 21: 149–70.

Calleo, David (2001). *Rethinking Europe's Future.* Princeton: Princeton University Press.

Campbell, John (2004). *Institutional Change and Globalization.* Princeton: Princeton University Press.

Caporaso, James, M. G. Cowles, and T. Risse (2001). *Transforming Europe: Europeanization and Domestic Change.* Ithaca: Cornell University Press.

Castells, Manuel (1996). *The Rise of the Network Society.* Oxford: Blackwell.

Checkel, Jeffrey (2005). "International Institutions and Socialization in Europe," *International Organization.* 59(4): 801–26.

Chilton, Patricia (1997). "Common, Collective, or Combined? Theories of Defense Integration in the European Union," in *The State of the European Union,* vol. 3, edited by C. Rhodes and S. Mazey. Boulder: Lynne Rienner.

Christiansen, Thomas, K. Jorgensen, and A. Wiener (1999). "The Social Construction of Europe," *Journal of European Public Policy.* 6(4): 528–44.

Clarke, Michael and P. Cornish (2002). "The European Defence Project and the Prague Summit," *International Affairs.* 78(4): 777–88.

Cogan, Charles (2001). *The Third Option: The Emancipation of European Defense, 1989–2000.* Westport: Praeger.

Cohen, Antonin, Y. Dezalay, and D. Marchetti (2007). "Esprits d'état, entrepreneurs d'Europe," *Actes de la recherche en sciences sociales.* 166/167: 5–13.

Cooper, Robert (2004). *The Breaking of Nations: Order and Chaos in the Twenty-First Century.* New York: Atlantic Monthly Press.

Cornish, Paul and G. Edwards (2001). "Beyond the EU/NATO Dichotomy: The Beginnings of an EU Strategic Culture," *International Affairs.* 77(3): 587–603.

Croft, Stuart (2000). "The EU, NATO, and Europeanisation: The Return of Architectural Debate," *European Security.* 9(3): 1–20.

Cross, Mai'a. K. D. (2006). *The European Diplomatic Corps: Diplomats and International Cooperation from Westphalia to Maastricht.* Houndmills: Palgrave.

Crowe, Brian (2003). "A Common Foreign Policy After Iraq?" *International Affairs.* 79(3): 533–46.

Dandeker, Christopher and L. Freedman (2002). "The British Armed Services," *Political Quarterly.* 73: 465–75.

De Schoutheete, Philippe (2004). "La cohérence par la défense, une autre lecture de la PESD," *Cahier de Chaillot #71.* Paris: Institut d'Études de Sécurité de l'Union Européenne.

Deak, Istvan (1990). *Beyond Nationalism: A Social and Political History of the Habsburg Officer Corps, 1848–1918.* Oxford: Oxford University Press.

Decup, Sabine Marie (1998). *France–Angleterre: Les relations militaires de 1945 à 1962*. Paris: Economica.

Deighton, Anne (2001). "European Union Policy," in *The Blair Effect*, edited by A. Seldon. London: Little, Brown, and Co.

Deutsch, Karl et al. (1957). *Political Community and the North Atlantic Area*. Princeton: Princeton University Press.

Dezalay, Yves (2007). "De la défense de l'environnement au développement durable: L'émergence d'un champ d'expertise des politiques européennes," *Actes de la recherche en sciences sociales*. 166/167: 66–79.

Dobbin, Frank (1994). *Forging Industrial Policy: The United States, Britain and France in the Railway Age*. Cambridge: Cambridge University Press.

Dorman, Andrew (2002). "European Adaptation to Expeditionary Warfare: Implications for the US Army," Working Paper, Strategic Studies Institute. Carlisle: US Army War College.

Dover, Robert (2005). "The Prime Minister and the Core Executive: A Liberal Intergovernmentalist Reading of UK Defence Policy Formulation," *British Journal of Politics and International Relations*. 7(4): 508–25.

Downing, Brian (1992). *The Military Revolution and Political Change: Origins of Democracy and Autocracy in Early Modern Europe*. Princeton: Princeton University Press.

Duchêne, François (1972). "Europe's Role in World Peace," in *Europe Tomorrow: Sixteen Europeans Look Ahead*. London: Fontana.

Duffield, John (1995). *Power Rules: The Evolution of NATO's Conventional Force Posture*. Stanford: Stanford University Press.

—— (1998). *World Power Forsaken: Political Culture, International Institutions, and German Security Policy after Unification*. Stanford: Stanford University Press.

Duke, Simon and H. Ojanen (2006). "Bridging Internal and External Security: Lessons from the European Security and Defence Policy," *Journal of European Integration*. 28(5): 477–94.

Dumoulin, André and E. Remacle (1998). *La communauté européenne de défense, phénix de la défense européenne*. Brussels: Bruylant.

—— R. Mathieu, and G. Sarlet (2003). *La politique européenne de sécurité et de défense: De l'opératoire à l'identitaire*. Brussels: Bruylant.

Eilstrup-Sangiovanni, Mette (2003). "Why a Common Security and Defence Policy is Bad for Europe," *Survival*. 45(3): 193–206.

—— and D. Verdier (2005). "European Integration as a Solution to War," *European Journal of International Relations*. 11(1): 99–135.

Ekengren, Magnus (2002). *The Time of European Governance.* Manchester: Manchester University Press.

Elliot, Lorraine and G. Cheeseman (eds.) (2004). *Forces for Good: Cosmopolitan Militaries in the 21st Century.* Manchester: Manchester University Press.

Eloranta, Jari (2004). "Warfare and Welfare: Understanding 19th and 20th Century Central Government Spending," Working Paper, Department of Economics. Coventry: University of Warwick.

Eriksson, Arita (2006). "Europeanization and Governance in Defence Policy: The Example of Sweden," *Stockholm Studies in Politics #117.* Stockholm: Stockholm University.

Ertman, Thomas (1997). *Birth of the Leviathan: Building States and Regimes in Medieval and Early Modern Europe.* Cambridge: Cambridge University Press.

Everts, Steve et al. (2004). *A European Way of War.* London: Centre for European Reform.

Faria, Fernanda (2004). "Crisis Management in Sub-Saharan Africa: The Role of the European Union," Occasional Paper. Paris: European Union Institute for Security Studies.

Finer, Samuel E. (1975). "State and Nation Building in Europe: The Role of the Military," in *The Formation of National States in Western Europe,* edited by C. Tilly. Princeton: Princeton University Press.

Finnemore, Martha (1996). "Norms, Culture, and World Politics: Insights from Sociology's Institutionalism," *International Organization.* 50(2): 325–47.

Fleckenstein, Bernhard (2000). "Germany: Forerunner of a Postnational Military," in *The Postmodern Military: Armed Forces After the Cold War,* edited by C. Moskos, J. Allen, and D. Segal. Oxford: Oxford University Press.

Fligstein, Neil (2001a). *The Architecture of Markets: An Economic Sociology of 21st Century Capitalist Societies.* Princeton: Princeton University Press.

—— (2001b). "Social Skills and the Theory of Fields," *Sociological Theory.* 19(2): 105–25.

—— (2008). *Euroclash: The EO, European Identity, and the Future of Europe.* Oxford: Oxford University Press.

Forster, Anthony (2005). *Armed Forces and Society in Europe.* Houndmills: Palgrave.

—— and A. Blair (2002). *The Making of Britain's EU Policy.* London: Longman.

Freedman, Lawrence (2001). "Defence," in *The Blair Effect: The Blair Government, 1997–2001,* edited by A. Seldon. London: Little, Brown, and Co.

Garton Ash, Timothy (2005). *Free World: America, Europe, and the Surprising Future of the West.* New York: Vintage Books.

Gautier, Louis (1999). *Mitterrand et son armée, 1990–1995.* Paris: Grasset.

Gegout, Catherine (2002). "The Quint: Acknowledging the Existence of a Big Four—US Directoire at the Heart of the European Union's Foreign Policy Decision-Making Process," *Journal of Common Market Studies.* 40: 331–44.

—— (2005). "Causes and Consequences of the EU's Military Intervention in the Democratic Republic of Congo (DRC): A Realist Explanation," *European Foreign Affairs Review.* 10(3): 427–43.

Georgakakis, Didier and M. de Lassalle (2007). "Genèse et structure d'un capital institutionnel européen: Les très hauts fonctionnaires de la Commission européenne," *Actes de la recherche en sciences sociales.* 166/167: 38–53.

Gellner, Ernest (1983). *Nations and Nationalism.* Ithaca: Cornell University Press.

Gheciu, Alexandra (2005). *NATO in the New Europe: The Politics of International Socialization after the Cold War.* Stanford: Stanford University Press.

Giddens, Anthony (1987). *The Nation State and Violence.* Berkeley: University of California Press.

Giegerich, Bastian (2006). *European Security and Strategic Culture: National Responses to the EU's Security and Defence Policy.* Baden–Baden: Nomos.

—— and E. Gross (2006). "Squaring the Circle? Leadership and Legitimacy in European Defence Cooperation," *International Politics.* 43(4): 500–9.

—— and W. Wallace (2004). "Not Such a Soft Power: The External Deployments of European Forces," *Survival.* 46(2): 163–82.

Ginsberg, Roy H (1989). *Foreign Policy Actions of the European Community: The Politics of Scale.* London: Lynne Rienner.

—— (2001). *The European Union in International Politics.* Lanham: Rowman & Littlefield.

Girardet, Raoul (1998). *La société militaire de 1815 à nos jours.* Paris: Perrin.

Glarbo, Kenneth (1999). "Wide-Awake Diplomacy: Reconstructing the Common Foreign and Security Policy of the European Union," *Journal of European Public Policy.* 6(4): 634–51.

Gnesotto, Nicole (1998). *La puissance et l'Europe.* Paris: Presses de Sciences Po.

Goffman, Erving (1974). *Frame Analysis.* Cambridge: Harvard University Press.

Grant, Charles (2002). "A European View on ESDP," in *Readings in European Security,* edited by K. Becher, M. Houben, and M. Emerson. Brussels/London: Center for European Policy Studies/International Institute for Security Studies.

Guiraudon, Virginie (2000). "L'espace sociopolitique européen, un champ encore en friche?" *Cultures et conflits.* 38/39: 7–37.

Haas, Ernst (1958). *The Uniting of Europe: Political, Social, and Economic Forces, 1950–1957*. Stanford: Stanford University Press.

Haas, Peter (1991). "Epistemic Communities and International Policy Coordination," *International Organization*. 46(1): 1–35.

Haine, Jean-Yves (2001). *L'Eurocorps: Processus de socialisation et construction d'une identité transnationale*. Paris: Centre d'études en sciences sociales de la Défense.

Heisbourg, François et al. (2000). *European Defence: Making it Work. Chaillot Paper* #42. Paris: Western European Union Institute for Security Studies.

Held, David (1999). *Global Transformations: Politics, Economics and Culture*. Stanford: Stanford University Press.

Héritier, Adrienne (1999). *Policy-Making and Diversity in Europe: Escape from Deadlock*. Cambridge: Cambridge University Press.

Heuser, Beatrice (1997). *NATO, Britain, France and the FRG: Nuclear Strategies and Forces for Europe, 1949–2000*. London: Macmillan.

Hill, Christopher (1993). "The Capability-Expectations Gap, or Conceptualizing Europe's International Role," *Journal of Common Market Studies*. 31(3): 305–28.

——— and W. Wallace (1996). "Introduction," in *The Actors in Europe's Foreign Policy*, edited by C. Hill. London: Routledge.

Hintze, Otto (1975). *The Historical Essays of Otto Hintze*. Oxford: Oxford University Press.

Hirst, Paul (2001). *War and Power in the 21st Century*. Cambridge: Polity.

Hobden, Stephen and J. M. Hobson (eds.) (2002). *Historical Sociology of International Relations*. Cambridge: Cambridge University Press.

Hocking, Brian (2002). "Gatekeepers and Boundary-Spanners: Thinking about Foreign Ministries in the European Union," in *Foreign Ministries in the European Union: Integrating Diplomat*, edited by B. Hocking and D. Spence. Houndmills: Palgrave.

——— and D. Spence (eds.) (2002). *Foreign Ministries in the European Union: Integrating Diplomats*. Houndmills: Palgrave.

Hoffmann, Stanley (1966). "Obstinate or Obsolete: the Fate of the Nation State and the Case of Western Europe," *Daedalus*. 95: 862–915.

——— (1995). *The European Sisyphus: Essays on Europe, 1964–94*. Boulder: Westview Press.

Hooghe, Liesbet (2002). *The European Commission and the Integration of Europe: Images of Governance*. Cambridge: Cambridge University Press.

Howorth, Jolyon (2000a). "Britain, France, and the European Defence Initiative," *Survival*. 42(2): 33–55.

Howorth, Jolyon (2000*b*). "European Integration and Defence: The Ultimate Challenge?" Chaillot Paper #43. Paris: WEU Institute for Security Studies.

—— (2001). "European Defence and the Changing Politics of the European Union: Hanging Together or Hanging Separately?" *Journal of Common Market Studies* 39: 765–89.

—— (2003). "Discourse, Ideas, and Epistemic Communities in European Security and Defence Policy," *West European Politics.* 27(1): 29–52.

—— (2004). "The European Union Draft Constitutional Treaty and the Future of the European Defence Initiative: A Question of Flexibility?" *European Foreign Affairs Review.* 9(4): 483–508.

—— (2007). *Security and Defence Policy in the European Union.* Houndmills: Palgrave.

Hunter, Robert and D. Farley (2002). *The European Security and Defence Policy: NATO's Companion or Competitor?* Santa Monica: RAND Corporation.

Huntington, Samuel (1957). *The Soldier and the State: The Theory and Politics of Civil-Military Relations.* Cambridge: Harvard University Press.

Hyde-Price, Adrian (2006). "Normative Power Europe: A Realist Critique," *Journal of European Public Policy.* 13(2): 217–34.

Irondelle, Bastien (2003*a*). "Europeanization Without the European Union? French Military Reforms, 1991–1996," *Journal of European Public Policy.* 10(2): 208–26.

—— (2003*b*). "Civil-Military Relations and the End of Conscription in France," *Security Studies.* 12(3): 157–87.

Jabko, Nicolas (2006). *Playing the Market: A Political Strategy for Uniting Europe, 1985–2005.* Ithaca: Cornell University Press.

Joana, Jean and A. Smith (2002). *Les commissaires européens: Technocrates, diplomates ou politiques?* Paris: Presses de Sciences Po.

Johnston, Alastair I. (1995). "Thinking about Strategic Culture," *International Security.* 19(4): 32–64.

Jones, Seth G. (2007). *The Rise of European Security Cooperation.* Cambridge: Cambridge University Press.

Jopp, Mathias (1999). "European Defence Policy: The Debate on Institutional Aspects," Working Paper. Bonn: Institut für Europäische Politik.

Judt, Tony (2006). *Postwar: A History of Europe Since 1945.* London: Penguin.

Kantorowicz, Ernst (1951). "Pro Patria Mori in Medieval Political Thought," *American Historical Review.* 56: 472–92.

Kassim, Hussein (2001). "Introduction," in *The National Co-ordination of EU Policy,* edited by H. Kassim, A. Menon, B. G. Peters, and V. Wright. Oxford: Oxford University Press.

Kassim, Hussein and B. G. Peters (2001). "Co-ordinating National Action in Brussels: A Comparative Perspective," in *The National Co-ordination of EU Policy*, edited by H. Kassim, A. Menon, B. G. Peters, and V. Wright. Oxford: Oxford University Press.

Katzenstein, Peter (ed.) (1996). *The Culture of National Security*. New York: Columbia University Press.

—— (2005). *A World of Regions: Asia and Europe in the American Imperium*. Ithaca: Cornell University Press.

Kauppi, Niilo (2003). "Bourdieu's Political Sociology and the Politics of European Integration," *Theory and Society*. 32(5–6): 775–89.

Keohane, Daniel (2002). *The EU and Armaments Co-operation*. London: Centre for European Reform.

Kier, Elizabeth (1997). *Imagining War: French and British Military Doctrine between the Wars*. Princeton: Princeton University Press.

King, Anthony (2003). *The European Ritual: Football and the New Europe*. London: Ashgate.

—— (2005). "Towards a Transnational Europe: The Case of the Armed Forces," *European Journal of Social Theory*. 8(3): 321–40.

Lascoumes, Pierre (1996). "Rendre gouvernable: De la traduction au transcodage," in *La gouvernabilité*, edited by CURAPP. Paris: Presses universitaires de France.

Lattimore, Owen (1962). *Nomads and Commissars: Mongolia Revisited*. Oxford: Oxford University Press.

Leonard, Mark (2005). *Why Europe Will Run the 21st Century*. New York: Public Affairs.

Lequesne, Christian and A. Smith (1997). "Union européenne et science politique: Ou en est le débat théorique?" *Cultures et Conflits*. 28: 7–31.

Lévi-Strauss, Claude (1961). *La pensée sauvage*. Paris: Plon.

Lewis, Jeffrey (2003). "Institutional Environments and Everyday EU Decision Making: Rationalist or Constructivist?" *Comparative Political Studies*. 36(1/2): 97–124.

Lindert, Peter (2004). *Growing Public: Social Spending and Economic Growth since the Eighteenth Century*. Cambridge: Cambridge University Press.

Lindley-French, Julian (2002). "In the Shade of Locarno? Why European Defence is Failing," *International Affairs*. 78: 789–811.

Manigart, Philippe (2001). "Europeans and a Common Defense Policy: A Comparative Analysis," in *Public Opinion and European Defense*, edited by J. Callaghan, F. Kernic, and P. Manigart. Garmisch-Partenkirchen: Peter Lang.

Mann, Michael (1986). *The Sources of Social Power*, Vol. I. Cambridge: Cambridge University Press.

Mann, Michael (1993). *The Sources of Social Power*, Vol. II. Cambridge: Cambridge University Press.

—— (1997). "Has Globalization Ended the Rise and Fall of Nation-State?" *Review of International Political Economy.* 4(3): 472–96.

Manners, Ian (2006). "Normative Power Europe Reconsidered: Beyond the Crossroads," *Journal of European Public Policy.* 13(2): 182–99.

Marks, Gary, F. Scharpf, P. Schmitter, and W. Streeck (1996). *Governance in the European Union.* London: Sage.

Martin, Andrew and G. Ross (1999). *The Brave New World of European Labor: European Trade Unions at the Millennium.* New York: Berhahn Books.

Mattli, Walter and A.-M. Slaughter (1998). "Revisiting the European Court of Justice," *International Organization.* 52(1): 177–209.

McCormick, John (2001). *Environmental Policy in the European Union.* Houndmills: Palgrave.

Mearsheimer, John (1990). "Back to the Future: Instability in Europe after the Cold War," *International Security.* 15(1): 5–56.

Medrano, Juan Diez (2003). *Framing Europe: Attitudes to European Integration in Germany, Spain and the United Kingdom.* Princeton: Princeton University Press.

Meiers, Franz-Josef (2001). "The Reform of the Budeswehr: Adaptation or Fundamental Renewal?" *European Security.* 10: 1–22.

Menon, Anand (2000). *France, NATO, and the Limits of Independence: The Politics of Ambivalence.* London: Macmillan.

—— (2003). "Why ESDP is Misguided and Dangerous for the Alliance," in *Defending Europe: The EU, NATO and the Quest for European Autonomy*, edited by J. Howorth and J. Keeler. New York: Palgrave.

—— (ed.) (2004). *Britain and European Integration: Views from Within.* Oxford: Blackwell.

Mérand, Frédéric (2003). "Dying for the Union? Military Officers and the European Defence Force," *European Societies.* 5(3): 253–82.

—— (2006). "Social Representations in the European Security and Defence Policy," *Cooperation and Conflict.* 41(2): 131–52.

—— (2007). "Strategic Partners, Different Strategies: Canada and the United States in the Transatlantic Security Community," in *The Changing Politics of European Security: Europe Alone?* edited by A. Sens and S. Gänzle. Houndmills: Palgrave.

—— and V. Pouliot (2008). "Le monde de Pierre Bourdieu: Éléments pour une théorie sociale des relations internationales," *Canadian Journal of Political Science.*

Merlingen, Michael and R. Ostrauskaite (2006). *European Union Peacebuilding and Policing: Governance and the European Security and Defence Policy.* London: Routledge.

Meyer, Christoph O. (2005). "Convergence Towards a European Strategic Culture? A Constructivist Framework for Explaining Changing Norms," *European Journal of International Relations.* 11(4): 523–49.

——(2006). *The Quest for a European Strategic Culture: Changing Norms on Security and Defence in the European Union.* Houndmills: Palgrave.

Milward, Alan (1992). *The European Rescue of the Nation-State.* London: Routledge.

Missiroli, Antonio (2003). "Euros for ESDP: Financing EU Operations," Occasional Paper #45. Paris: EU Institute for Security Studies.

Monnet, Jean (1976). *Mémoires.* Paris: Fayard.

Moravcsik, Andrew (1993). "Armaments Among Allies: European Weapons Collaboration, 1975–1985," in *Double-Edged Diplomacy: International Bargaining and Domestic Politics,* edited by H. Jacobsen, P. Evans, and R. Putnam. Berkeley: University of California Press.

——(1998). *The Choice for Europe: Social Purpose and State Power from Messina to Maastricht.* Ithaca: Cornell University Press.

——(2003). "Striking a New Transatlantic Bargain," *Foreign Affairs.* 82: 74–89.

Morgan, Patrick M. (2003). "NATO and European Security: the Creative Use of an International Organization," *Journal of Strategic Studies.* 26(3): 49–74.

Mörth, Ulrika (2004). *Organizing European Cooperation: The Case of Armaments.* Lanham: Rowman & Littlefield.

Moskos, Charles, J. A. Allen, and D. Segal (eds.) (2000). *The Postmodern Military: Armed Forces After the Cold War.* Oxford: Oxford University Press.

Neumann, Iver. B. (2005). "To Be a Diplomat," *International Studies Perspectives.* 6(1): 72–93.

Niblett, Robin and W. Wallace (2001). *Rethinking European Order: West European Responses, 1989–97.* Houndmills: Palgrave.

Nuttall, Simon J. (1992). *European Political Co-operation.* Oxford: Oxford University Press.

Ojanen, Hanna (2006). "The EU and NATO: Two Competing Models for a Common Defence Policy," *Journal of Common Market Studies.* 44(1): 57–76.

Olsen, Johan P. (2002). "The Many Faces of Europeanization," *Journal of Common Market Studies.* 40(5): 921–52.

Parker, Geoffrey (1996). *The Military Revolution: Military Innovation and the Rise of the West, 1500–1800.* Cambridge: Cambridge University Press.

Parsons, Craig (2004). *A Certain Idea of Europe.* Ithaca, NY: Cornell University Press.

Patten, Christopher (2001). "In Defence of Europe's Foreign Policy," *Financial Times*. 16 October.

Paulmier, Thierry (1997). *L'armée française et les opérations de maintien de la paix*. Paris: LGDJ.

Peled, A. (2000). "The Politics of Language in Multiethnic Militaries: The Case of Oriental Jews in the Israel Defense Forces, 1950–59," *Armed Forces and Society*. 26: 587–605.

Pierson, Paul (1996). "The Path to European Integration: A Historical-Institutionalist Analysis," *Comparative Political Studies*. 29(2): 123–63.

Posen, Barry (1984). *The Sources of Military Doctrine: France, Britain, and Germany Between the World Wars*. Ithaca: Cornell University Press.

—— (1993). "Nationalism, the Mass Army, and Military Power," *International Security*. 18(2): 80–124.

—— (2004). "ESDP and the Structure of World Power," *The International Spectator*. XXXIX(1): 5–17.

—— (2006). "European Union Security and Defense Policy: Response to Unipolarity?" *Security Studies*. 15(2): 149–86.

Powell, Walter and P. DiMaggio (eds.) (1991). *The New Institutionalism in Organizational Analysis*. Chicago: University of Chicago Press.

Quinlan, Michael (2001). *European Defense Cooperation: Asset or Threat to NATO?* Washington: Woodrow Wilson Center Press.

Radaelli, Claudio (2006). "Europeanization," in *Advances in European Union Studies*, edited by M. Cini and A. Bourne. Houndmills: Palgrave.

Ralston, David B. (1966). *The Army of the Republic. The Place of the Military in the Political Evolution of France, 1871–1914*. Cambridge: MIT Press.

Rathbun, Brian (2004). *Partisan Interventions: European Party Politics and Peace Enforcement in the Balkans*. Ithaca: Cornell University Press.

Rees, Wyn (1998). *The Western European Union at the Crossroads: Between Trans-Atlantic Solidarity and European Integration*. Boulder: Westview Press.

—— (2001). "Preserving the Security of Europe," in *Britain and Defence, 1945–2000: A Policy Re-evaluation*, edited by A. Dorman, S. Croft, W. Rees, and M. Uttley. London: Longman.

Regelsberger, Elfriede and W. Wessels (2007). "The Evolution of the Common Foreign and Security Policy: A Case of an Imperfect Ratchet Fusion," in *The European Union in the Wake of Eastern Enlargement*, edited by O. Croci and A. Verdun. Manchester: Manchester University Press.

Risse, Thomas (2004). "Social Constructivism and European Integration," in *European Integration Theory*, edited by A. Wiener and T. Diez. Oxford: Oxford University Press.

Risse-Kappen, Thomas (1995). *Cooperation Among Democracies: The European Influence on US Foreign Policy.* Princeton: Princeton University Press.

Rumford, Chris (2002). *The European Union: A Political Sociology.* Oxford: Blackwell.

Rynning, Sten (2003). "The European Union: Towards a Strategic Culture?" *Security Dialogue.* 34(4): 479–96.

Salmon, Trevor C. and A. J. K. Shepherd (2003). *Toward a European Army: A Military Power in the Making?* Boulder: Lynne Rienner.

Sandholtz, Wayne and A. S. Sweet (eds.) (1998). *European Integration and Supranational Governance.* Oxford: Oxford University Press.

Sarotte, Mary Elise (2001). "German Military Reform and European Security," *Adelphi Paper.* London: International Institute for Strategic Studies.

Sauder, A. (1995). *Souveränität und Integration: Französische und deutsche europäischer Sicherheit nach dem End des Kalten Krieges, 1990–1993.* Baden-Baden: Nomos.

Schake, Kori (2002). *Constructive Duplication.* London: Centre for European Reform.

Shaw, Martin (1997). "The State of Globalization: Towards a Theory of State Transformation," *Review of International Political Economy.* 4(3): 497–513.

—— (2000). *Theory of the Global State: Globality as Unfinished Revolution.* Cambridge: Cambridge University Press.

Schimmelfenning, Frank (2004). *The EU, NATO, and the Integration of Europe: Rules and Rhetoric.* Cambridge: Cambridge University Press.

Schmitt, Burkard (2000). "From Cooperation to Integration: Defence and Aerospace Industries in Europe," Chaillot Paper #40. Paris: WEU Institute for Security Studies.

—— (2003). "The European Union and Armaments: Getting a Bigger Bang for the Euro," Chaillot Paper #63. Paris: EU Institute for Security Studies.

—— (2004). "Les capacités: l'Union, combien de divisions?" in *La politique de sécurité et de défense de l'UE: Les cinq premières années,* edited by N. Gnesotto. Paris: Institut d'études de sécurité de l'Union européenne.

Scholte, Jan-Aart (2000). *Globalization: A Critical Introduction.* Houndmills: Palgrave.

Shore, Cris (2000). *Building Europe: The Cultural Politics of European Integration.* London: Routledge.

Siedentop, Larry (2002). *Democracy in Europe.* New York: Columbia University Press.

Singer, P. W. (2002). *Corporate Warriors: The Rise of the Privatized Military Industry.* Ithaca: Cornell University Press.

Sjursen, Helene (2006). "The EU as a 'Normative' Power: How Can This Be?" *Journal of European Public Policy.* 13(2): 235–51.

Skocpol, Theda (1992). *Protecting Soldiers and Mothers: The Political Origins of Social Policy in the United States.* Cambridge: Harvard University Press.

Slaughter, Anne-Marie (2004). *A New World Order.* Princeton: Princeton University.

Sloan, Stanley R. (2002). *NATO, the European Union and the Atlantic Community: The Transatlantic Bargain Challenged.* Lanham: Rowman & Littlefield.

Smith, Hazel (2002). *European Union Foreign Policy: What it is and What it Does.* London: Pluto Press.

Smith, Michael E. (2004). *Europe's Foreign and Security Policy: The Institutionalization of Cooperation.* Cambridge: Cambridge University Press.

Snyder, Jack (1989). *The Ideology of the Offensive: Military Decision-Making and the Disasters of 1914.* Ithaca: Cornell University Press.

Spence, David (2002). "The Evolving Role of Foreign Ministries in the Conduct of European Union Affairs," in *Foreign Ministries in the European Union: Integrating Diplomats,* edited by B. Hocking and D. Spence. Houndmills: Palgrave.

Spruyt, Hendrik (1994). *The Sovereign State and Its Competitors.* Princeton: Princeton University Press.

Steenbergen, Marco and G. Marks (2004). "Models of Political Conflict in the European Union," in *European Integration and Political Conflict,* edited by G. Marks and M. Steenbergen. Cambridge: Cambridge University Press.

Strange, Susan (1996). *The Retreat of the State: The Diffusion of Power in the World Economy.* Cambridge: Cambridge University Press.

Telò, Mario (2005). *Europe, a Civilian Power? European Union, Global Governance, World Order.* Houndmills: Palgrave.

Terriff, Terry (2003). "The CJTF Concept and the Limits of European Autonomy," in *Defending Europe: The EU, NATO and the Quest for European Autonomy,* edited by J. Howorth and J. Keeler. New York: Palgrave.

——(2004). "NATO: Warfighters or Cosmopolitan Warriors?" in *Forces for Good: Cosmopolitan Militaries in the 21st Century,* edited by L. Elliot and G. Cheeseman. Manchester: Manchester University Press.

Thomas, James P. (2000). *The Military Challenges of Transatlantic Coalitions.* Oxford/London: Oxford University Press/International Institute of Strategic Studies.

Thomas, Daniel C. (2001). *The Helsinki Effect: International Norms, Human Rights, and the Demise of Communism.* Princeton: Princeton University Press.

Tilly, Charles (1985). "War Making and State Making as Organized Crime," in *Bringing the State Back In,* edited by D. Rueschmeyer, P. Evans, and T. Skocpol. Cambridge: Cambridge University Press.

——(1992). *Coercion, Capital and European States, AD 990–1992.* Oxford: Blackwell.

Todorov, Tzvetan (2003). *Le nouveau désordre mondial: Réflexions d'un européen.* Paris: Robert Laffont.

Tonra, Ben (2003). "Constructing the CFSP: The Utility of a Cognitive Approach," *Journal of Common Market Studies.* 41(4): 731–56.

Treacher, Adrian (2001). "Europe as a Power Multiplier for French Security Policy: Strategic Consistency, Tactical Adaptation," *European Security.* 10(1): 22–44.

——(2004). "From Civilian Power to Military Power: the EU's Resistible Transformation," *European Foreign Affairs Review.* 9(1): 49–66.

Tuschhoff, Christian. (1999). "Alliance Cohesion and Peaceful Change in NATO," in *Imperfect Unions: Security Institutions over Time and Space,* edited by R. Keohane, H. Haftendorn, and C. Wallander. Oxford: Oxford University Press.

Unterseher, Lutz (1999). *Europe's Armed Forces at the Millennium: A Case Study of Change in France, the United Kingdom, and Germany.* Cambridge: Project on Defense Alternatives, International Study Group on Alternative Security Policy.

Van Creveld, Martin (1999). *The Rise and Decline of the State.* Cambridge: Cambridge University Press.

Vauchez, Antoine (2007). "Une élite d'intermédiaires: Genèse d'un capital juridique européen (1950–70)," *Actes de la recherche en sciences sociales.* 166/167: 54–65.

Vennesson, Pascal (2000). "Bombarder pour convaincre? Puissance aérienne, rationalité limitée et diplomatie coercitive au Kosovo," *Cultures et Conflits.* 37: 23–59.

Vial, Philippe (2002). "Une place à part. Les militaires et les relations extérieures de la France en temps de paix depuis 1870," *Matériaux pour l'histoire de notre temps.* 65: 41–7.

Wagner, Anne-Catherine (2005). *Vers une Europe syndicale: Une enquête sur la Confédération européenne des syndicats.* Paris: Croquant.

Wallace, William (1986). "Defence: The Defence of Sovereignty, or the Defence of Germany?" in *Partners and Rivals in Western Europe: Britain, France, and Germany,* edited by R. Morgan and C. Bray. London: Gower.

Wallace, Helen and W. Wallace (2000). *Policy-Making in the European Union.* Oxford: Oxford University Press.

Wallander, Celeste, H. Haftendorn, and R. Keohane (1999). "Introduction," in *Imperfect Unions: Security Institutions over Time and Space,* edited by R. Keohane et al. Oxford: Oxford University Press.

Walt, Stephen (1987). *The Origins of Alliances.* Ithaca: Cornell University Press.

Waltz, Kenneth (1979). *Theory of International Politics.* Reading: Addison-Wesley.

Webber, Mark, S. Croft, J. Howorth, T. Terriff, and E. Krahmann (2004). "The Governance of European Security," *Review of International Studies.* 30(1): 3–26.

Weber, Eugen (1974). *Peasants into Frenchmen: The Modernization of Rural France, 1871–1914.* Stanford: Stanford University Press.

Weber, Max (1978). *Economy and Society.* Berkeley: University of California Press.

Weber, Steve (1992). "Shaping the Postwar Balance of Power: Multilateralism in NATO," *International Organization.* 46(3): 633–80.

Weiler, Joseph (1999). *The Constitution of Europe: Do the New Clothes Have an Emperor?* Cambridge: Cambridge University Press.

Wendt, Alexander (1994). "Collective Identity Formation and the International State," *American Political Science Review.* 88(2): 384–96.

——(1999). *Social Theory of International Politics.* Cambridge: Cambridge University Press.

Wessels, Wolfgang (1997). "An Ever Closer Fusion? A Dynamic Macropolitical View on Integration Processes," *Journal of Common Market Studies.* 35(2): 267–99.

White, Brian (2001). *Understanding European Foreign Policy.* Houndmills: Palgrave.

Whitman, Richard (1999). "Amsterdam's Unfinished Business? The Blair Government's Initiative and the Future of the Western European Union," Occasional Paper. Paris: Western European Institute for Security Studies.

Williams, Michael. C. (2006). *Culture and Security: The Reconstruction of Security in the Post-Cold War Era.* London: Routledge.

Winslow, Donna and P. Everts (2001). "It's not a Question of Muscle: Cultural Interoperability for NATO," in *A History of NATO: The First Fifty Years,* edited by G. Schmidt. Houndmills: Palgrave.

Yost, David. S. (2003). "The US-European Capabilities Gap and the Prospects for ESDP," in *Defending Europe: The EU, NATO and the Quest for European Autonomy,* edited by J. Howorth and J. Keeler. New York: Palgrave.

Young, Thomas-Durrell (2001). "Post-Cold War NATO Force Structure Planning and the Vexatious Issue of Multinational Land Forces," in *A History of NATO: The First Fifty Years,* edited by G. Schmidt. Houndmills: Palgrave.

Index